FACE

BY

Pixiwoo

For Mum, without your love and support
none of this would have been possible.

FACE

MAKE-UP • SKINCARE • BEAUTY

SAM AND NIC CHAPMAN

Published by Blink Publishing
3.25, The Plaza,
535 Kings Road,
Chelsea Harbour,
London, SW10 0SZ

www.blinkpublishing.co.uk

facebook.com/blinkpublishing
twitter.com/blinkpublishing

HB – 978-1-910536-74-2
Special edition – 978-1-911274-54-4

A CIP catalogue of this book is available from the British Library.

Printed and bound in Italy.

1 3 5 7 9 10 8 6 4 2

Text copyright © Samantha Chapman and Nicola Haste/Pixiwoo Limited, 2016
Images © Sam and Nic Chapman, Real Techniques, James Lincoln, Simon Songhurst, Elisabeth Hoff and Shutterstock.
Design by Type & Numbers Creative. www.typeandnumbers.com

Papers used by Blink Publishing are natural, recyclable products made from wood grown in sustainable forests.
The manufacturing processes conform to the environmental regulations of the country of origin.

Every reasonable effort has been made to trace copyright holders of material reproduced in this book,
but if any have been inadvertently overlooked the publishers would be glad to hear from them.

Blink Publishing is an imprint of the Bonnier Publishing Group
www.bonnierpublishing.co.uk

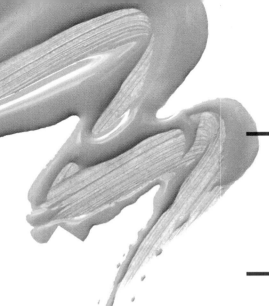

FACE

APP BY

Pixiwoo

THE ULTIMATE MAKE-UP AND BEAUTY GUIDE ON YOUR SCREEN!

Create the perfect look for every occasion with the Face App by Pixiwoo! The dynamic duo, Sam and Nic Chapman, share their extensive beauty knowledge and make-up expertise with exclusive digital content. From never-before-seen video tutorials, pictures and helpful tips, to special features such as the Selfie Booth, the Face App by Pixiwoo will help you achieve the incredible looks Sam and Nic are known for.

To access all this exclusive content, download the free app from the iTunes App Store or Google Play Store, launch the app and point your device's camera at the pages with the special phone icon (right) on them. Here all of Pixiwoo's advice and special features will come to life on your screen!

*The Face App by Pixiwoo requires an Internet connection to be downloaded and can be used on iPhone, iPad or Android devices. For direct links to download the app and further information, visit www.blinkpublishing.co.uk

SCAN THIS PAGE NOW FOR YOUR FIRST VIDEO!

FOR THE ULTIMATE FACE EXPERIENCE DON'T FORGET TO USE YOUR FREE AND UNIQUE PIXIWOO COLOUR WHEEL FOUND IN THE APP'S MAIN MENU

CONTENTS

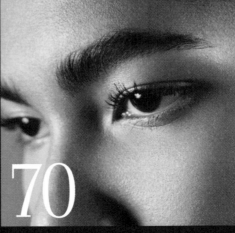
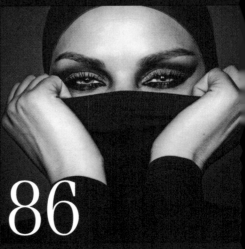

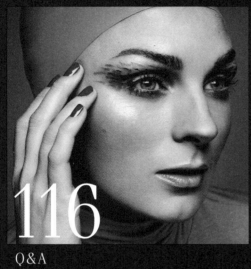
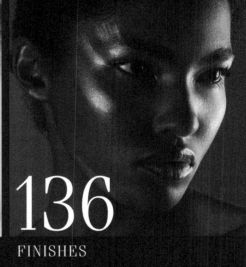
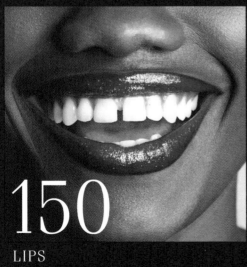

SAM & NIC

We have been educating women and men of all ages in the art of make-up for over 20 years. We developed Pixiwoo on social media back in 2008.

Pixiwoo was born out of our hard-earned knowledge and passion for make-up and we never imagined it would become our actual career. The success of our channel has enabled us to branch out in many areas.

We have taught hundreds of new make-up artists and we are always inspired by our students' enthusiasm and passion for make-up. We decided to use our knowledge of what people need to learn, to produce an easy-to-follow book that breaks down facial make-up and how to apply it, along with application techniques and our anecdotes and tips.

We wanted to get back to basics and assist beginners or students of the industry and also offer opinions and tips to working make-up artists.

We wanted to also incorporate our social media background and include interactive apps for extra product information, colour theory assistance and brand-new tutorials created especially for you.

You will learn more about us personally along with our opinions on the best products and also the techniques we normally edit out of our tutorials. You may wonder why we select certain products and tools for our tutorial videos and this book will tell you.

We have loved compiling our knowledge for you and if you are a total make-up beginner and are unsure of where to start then this book will be your companion. If you are just setting out in the industry we will offer you insider tips and advice for your journey.

We hope you enjoy!

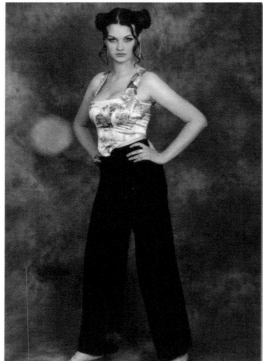

SAM

I always knew I wanted to do something involving make-up and creativity. As with most siblings, Nic and I squabbled regularly. Nic was the annoying little sister who enjoyed nothing better than trying to wind me up or embarrass me. The only thing that united us was our love of make-up. We loved to watch our mum apply her own make-up and took a great interest in our auntie's career as a make-up artist.

In 1993, after leaving school, I enrolled in a two-year BTEC course in media make-up before moving to London to assist our aunt. I was excited to get away from rural Norfolk and be independent. I began working on a make-up counter, which gave me confidence with different skin types and tones. I moved to a make-up studio in London where I created suitable looks while working fast.

After two years I began working for MAC in the Carnaby Street Pro Store and later became part of their Pro Team. I travelled extensively to create high-fashion looks for the various fashion weeks and assisted top make-up artists, including Val Garland, Charlotte Tilbury, Sharon Dowsett and Tom Pecheux. Life was pretty hectic but I was really focused on building up my personal portfolio so I would test with other creatives. I also did freelance work including bridal make-up as I was always conscious of having a back-up plan.

In 2003 I got my first agent and was soon booked for magazines and celebrity shoots. I left MAC and worked part-time for Chanel. A year later I had my first daughter, Lily. I continued to work freelance, including doing the make-up for artists at MTV and teaching at a make-up school.

Shortly before the birth of my second daughter, Olivia, I started the Pixiwoo YouTube channel. Nic's childhood nickname was Pixi and my email address then included the word 'Pixiwoo'. I used the name without thinking about how it would become our brand's logo. We like it, though, and there isn't much else out there similar to it.

My first tutorial created a look for a client who wanted a smoky eye. I felt writing the information wouldn't really give her a feel for it – plus I hated to write – so I filmed it instead. The client loved it and more people started to watch and request looks. It started to get really popular and I couldn't manage the workload. By then Nic and I had grown closer and the time we'd spent apart had made us appreciate each other. Nic was always very supportive and was also working in the industry so I asked her if she would like to join me. For two years we worked solidly on the channel, trying to build its popularity. I created tutorials that worked better with my features while Nic's suited her style and look.

The hard work got us noticed and in 2010 Real Techniques approached us. I became Artistic Consultant initially and helped them create a new, different type of make-up brush that performed exceptionally well at an affordable price. The brush range was based on our growing social media success. In 2013, when Nic was able to devote more energy to the brand, we became joint Artistic Consultants. Real Techniques has gone on to become the most popular make-up brush in the UK. It's also now currently the fastest growing make-up brush brand in the US.

We continue to push our brand and never take any of our opportunities for granted. We have worked so hard to build Pixiwoo and we try and take each day as it comes. We still have our fights and have very different ways of approaching situations but we always pull together and make a great team.

NICOLA

I was never really academic at school. I loved sports and art but as we grew up in rural Norfolk I was more interested in being outdoors with my friends. I had imagined I would be a nurse as I loved caring for people and this seemed like a natural progression for me.

When I eventually left school I still wasn't quite sure what to do next. Our mum's sister, Maggie, is a successful make-up artist and I loved listening to her talk about her glamorous clients and decided that this might be a fun industry to work in. Sam had already gone on to college to study make-up, and she encouraged me to give it a try. I studied a BTEC National Diploma at college and had a great two years but I still needed extra training and guidance. I don't think you ever really learn until you are in the industry.

I assisted my aunt and also gained valuable work experience at Nicky Clarke and Jo Hansford, both premium hairdressers in London. Based on my good work ethic they both offered me a job, but I was focused on make-up. I returned to Norfolk and landed a job for Estée Lauder working on the counter and gradually worked my way up to counter manager. I heard that there

was a MAC store coming to Norwich and working for a sister brand helped me to get an interview.

I was so excited and I can still remember the make-up I wore. A combination of So There Jade and Minted eyeliner, a vibrant green mascara called Boston Fern and a baby pink lipstick called Snob. It was a winning combination and I became an assistant manager.

I remained in this position for four years and made some great friends before becoming a supervisor at the MAC Pro Store in Carnaby Street, London, for three years. I would often freelance in the evenings – bridal work, drag make-up and editorial work. Then I joined Illamasqua in Selfridges.

In 2008 Sam told me that she had started recording make-up tutorials on YouTube and had begun to get lots of requests for looks. She asked if I wanted to help create some tutorials. Sam never really had a massive plan but we decided to create fun and informative content. I really enjoyed helping her but it was hard working full time and freelancing too. I decided that I would return home to Norfolk and give this YouTube thing a go! I knew I could always fall back on bridal make-up work.

We started creating looks for the channel and at the weekend we worked together as bridal make-up artists to earn some money. This was the first time in years we had been in each other's presence regularly but the time apart had drawn us closer.

I soon met my husband, Ian, and I knew that Norfolk was where I wanted to be so Sam and I focused really hard on the Pixiwoo channel. In 2010 we were approached by Real Techniques to help create a new type of make-up brush. I sadly had two miscarriages and just needed to focus on myself. I just helped behind the scenes at Real Techniques. Fortunately, Ian and I went on to have two beautiful children, Harry and Edie. I then joined the Real Techniques team with Sam as an Artistic Consultant while creating weekly tutorials for Pixiwoo.

We never like to plan too far ahead and take each day as it comes. We know each other's strengths and also when the other is struggling. Every week brings a new challenge but we deal with it together.

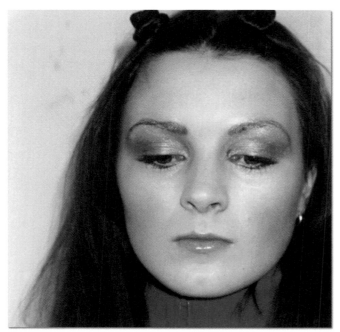

*"The right tools are just as important
as the make-up itself."*
———————— *Bobbi Brown*

TOOLS

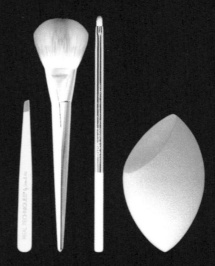

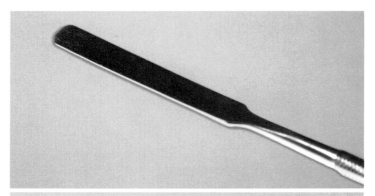

WHAT TOOLS YOU NEED DEPENDS ON YOUR CIRCUMSTANCES. A MAKE-UP ARTIST WORKING IN THE INDUSTRY WILL HAVE A DIFFERENT SET OF REQUIREMENTS FROM SOMEONE WHO NEEDS THE FUNDAMENTALS TO GET THEM THROUGH THE DAY. WE'LL TAKE YOU THROUGH SOME GREAT IDEAS SO YOU CAN PICK WHAT WORKS BEST FOR YOU.

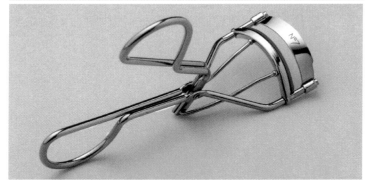

BASIC TOOLS

Nobody has one tone to their skin and, although it's unrealistic for everyone to purchase multiple foundations, you can often get the perfect shade by mixing from a variety of colours, just as an artist would do.

Keep a small palette in your kit so you can mix shades and products, either a professional palette or one from a good art department. Always go for a transparent or plain white palette.

A spatula is useful for adding cream, powder or gel products to the palette.

Tweezers have multiple uses, including hair removal, applying individual or strip lashes or for picking up adornments such as sequins or crystals.

Lash curlers can transform a look and enhance the shape of the eye no end. There are a variety of options (see Lashes, p. 126).

Disposable applicators should be kept at hand for applying to other people, mainly mascara. Never double dip your disposable mascara wand. Always use a fresh wand for each eye to prevent cross-contamination. Disposables can be purchased online in bulk if needed.

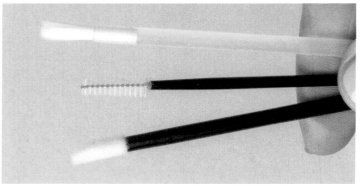

STORAGE

Good storage is vital to keep and transport your essentials hygienically and to ensure you can easily access what you need. First, let's look at make-up expiration dates. Old products can contain harmful levels of bacteria that can cause some pretty alarming infections.

Some liquids, such as moisturiser and foundation, are easy to spot when they are past their best. The packaging expands or has condensation marks and the content separates. Products which have a high level of water or natural plant derivatives are hot contenders for bacterial growth. Powders such as blusher and eye shadow have a longer shelf life, but speed of bacterial growth will be increased by repeatedly using a contaminated brush or sponge.

Next to the ingredients listing you will see an opened jar symbol which will include a number followed by the letter 'M'. The 'M' stands for 'months'. For example, a product may have the symbol 9M. This means you should throw it out nine months after opening.

Don't keep your products in your bathroom. The heat and humidity presents the perfect breeding environment for bacteria. Likewise, don't be tempted to keep your products in the fridge. The extreme temperature affects the stability and performance of the ingredients.

Keep skincare and make-up in a dark, cool location to maximise their shelf life. Mini storage drawers and units that have compartments to divide up your products make it easy to view and select them. You can separate products into colour, brands or style (depending on how organised you are!).

Palettes are the best way of coordinating and selecting your colours, either pre-stocked with colours or empty and magnetic which you fill with your own pans of eye shadows and blushers.

These often have a transparent lid for ease of viewing. We like to label these to differentiate similar colours.

Lipstick shades are often the most frustrating products to locate when jumbled in your bag. We have found the easiest way to store these is with the use of plastic pill cases. These have compartments into which you can decant lipsticks and label. We use a different case for every variety – reds, corals, pinks, etc. This makes life so much easier!

OLD PRODUCTS CAN CONTAIN *HARMFUL LEVELS* OF BACTERIA THAT *CAN CAUSE* SOME PRETTY *ALARMING INFECTIONS*.

Professional cases can often be quite pricey. For years we have used a medium-sized suitcase with wheels and an extendable handle. We separate our products into transparent zip-up bags for ease of access.

Brush belts are great for working in the industry. Working on location you will often find yourself in a dimly lit room or under fluorescent lights which alter the colour of your products. You can purchase your own portable lighting online. The kits fold down to a manageable size. The light bulbs replicate natural daylight and will illuminate the face and make-up to make your job a lot easier.

These have become popular with consumers in the last ten years. Maybe this has something to do with the rise of social media channels such as Pixiwoo where people can see how to use them.

Good brushes are not cheap, but they are an absolute necessity for longevity and precise application. Of course, the warmth of your fingers can be a great help when blending creams and liquids but brushes are the key to an immaculately executed look.

The confusingly large range of brushes can be categorised into two main types by bristles: synthetic and natural-hair.

Synthetic bristles are usually made of tacklon or nylon fibres. The bristles feel slightly more coated and have more of a sheen. The bristles are less porous meaning that cream, liquid and gel product will remain on the tips, allowing a longer play time.

Natural-hair brushes are made from a variety of hair types, often mixed, usually sable, pony, squirrel, badger, mink or goat. They feel flexible, soft and pick up more product while ensuring easy blending. They can be used with creams but perform better with powder.

The shape of the brush you select has a huge impact on the finish of your make-up and there are a bafflingly large number of styles available.

Fluffier brushes will lay down less product and create a very natural finish – good for blending or sweeping over products in a sheer wash.

Firmer, compact brushes pick up more product and allow for a precise application. Good for eyeshadow before blending or for creating a heavier impact. Looser, less compact brushes create

a natural finish with foundation. A flat or firm brush will create a full, more flawless finish.

Blended or duo-fibre brushes mix natural and synthetic hair. They often appear darker (usually black) at the base and have white tips. Use with liquid or powder. The natural hair provides a firm base and holds extra product, while the synthetic white tips softly buff the product off the skin. Use product sparingly to avoid streaking.

Sponges can be used to apply base and are either latex or polyurethane foam (good for latex allergies). They give a buildable, smooth coverage and are often curved to make it easy to get to all the contours of the face.

> *GOOD BRUSHES* ARE *NOT CHEAP,* BUT THEY ARE AN *ABSOLUTE NECESSITY* FOR LONGEVITY AND *PRECISE APPLICATION.*

THE *SHAPE OF THE BRUSH* YOU SELECT HAS A *HUGE IMPACT* ON THE *FINISH* OF YOUR MAKE-UP.

Dirty brushes harbour bacteria that cause skin infections or aggravate blemishes and acne. A brush full of old make-up will also shed hair, perform poorly and not last long.

Use a mild shampoo to clean make-up brushes and remove product residue. However, this has no anti-bacterial properties, so rinse the brush and then use a professional brush cleanser. Usually inexpensive, these are available in large quantities for multiple usage. They contain alcohol which kills bacteria and various proteins which help to condition and protect the hairs.

Clean your brushes at least three times a week if they are just being used on yourself and you have no skin conditions or blemishes. Otherwise, clean after every use.

First pour a small amount of cleanser into a glass and dip the brush in from the tips to halfway down the hairs.

Gently circle the brush onto a dry cloth or thick tissue to remove make-up. Be sure not to get the base of the brush hairs wet as this can loosen the glue which secures the hairs.

Ensure you reshape the brush hairs and leave them out to air dry naturally either on their side or hanging upside down. Never stand them up straight to dry as water may seep into the glue at the base.

The alcohol in brush cleanser means hairs dry off quicker and you can use them again within a few minutes.

So, out of the hundreds of brush variations which are essential?

DIRTY BRUSHES HARBOUR BACTERIA THAT CAUSE SKIN INFECTIONS OR AGGRAVATE BLEMISHES AND ACNE.

SKIN BRUSHES

This is often the hardest area to get right but get the skin correct and everything else will fall into place. A good foundation brush changes how your base looks and performs.

Flexible, looser-styled brushes are best for a sheer base of foundation that mimics your natural skin. Stippling brushes and duo-fibre brushes pick up less product and have a larger surface area to distribute product widely. Use a sweeping circular movement to buff the product into the skin, letting the tips of the brush do all the work. You can build product with this style of brush after the initial wash of colour has been buffed in.

Firmer, more compact brushes are best for medium-to-full cover. These have a more solid look and feel and are less flexible. They pick up more product and apply foundation in a condensed, smaller area giving you a fuller cover. You can build and blend with this style of brush but keep a stippling brush at hand for the contours of the face.

Foundation brushes are synthetic or have synthetic tips. You can also use a real-hair brush but it will absorb more product.

Sponge coverage can also be altered. A damp sponge dilutes foundation slightly and helps to achieve a sheer finish. A dry sponge will give a fuller cover.

Concealer brushes are crucial to a flawless finish and come in different styles. Fluffy brushes are used on the delicate skin around the eyes or on slight colour discolouration. They buff the product in without dragging the skin and blend into your foundation seamlessly.

Firmer, flatter brushes are best for blemishes or areas which require a fuller cover. Use the flat of a synthetic brush to pat in the concealer and then the tip of the brush to blend the edges.

A GOOD *FOUNDATION BRUSH* CHANGES HOW *YOUR BASE LOOKS AND PERFORMS.*

EYE BRUSHES

You can use both synthetic and natural-hair brushes on the eye area. You may prefer a synthetic brush with a cream and a natural-hair brush with powder, but in general, use a flatter, firm brush to lay down the initial product as it will push the product exactly where required. It is also great for building product and deepening tone.

Fluffy blending brushes are essential to blend a gradient of colour to perfection. Short-haired brushes will provide a dramatic blend and are good with products that require quick blending due to their fast drying time. A long, flexible-haired brush provides a softer blend. Product falls out a lot so be sure to give them a tap to remove excess powder before blending.

Some eye brushes are larger for quick application and to cover a broader area. Smaller eye brushes will be better for a smaller eye area or for more intricate colour placement.

Fine liner brushes or angled brushes are good for lining the eyes. The shorter the brush hair, the more control you will have over product placement. A more confident hand may prefer a longer, fine liner to create a sweeping feline flick.

Angled brushes are firmer and give better control over placement. The pointed end also helps you to create a sharper edge with your liner flick.

You can also use the same style of liner brush and angled brush on the brows. A double-sided brush comb is useful, with a firm bristle side to brush through brows and a fine tooth comb on the opposite side to separate lashes.

LIP BRUSHES

Some people prefer to apply their lipstick or gloss directly from the bullet. When applying to others it's more hygienic to use a lip brush. They are often retractable or have a case to cover the tip for transportation. Often these are synthetic brushes to avoid product absorption.

FINISHING BRUSHES

These are your larger powder, bronzer, contour and blush brushes and can be synthetic or natural-hair. The bigger the brush the sheerer the finish. To achieve a good contour use a firmer brush, ideally with an angle or squared-off edges, as they sit comfortably in the contours.

Kabuki brushes are short-stemmed with densely packed hairs and are commonly kept in the handbag for powder touch-ups.

THE *BIGGER THE BRUSH* THE *SHEERER THE FINISH*. TO ACHIEVE A *GOOD CONTOUR* USE A *FIRMER BRUSH*, IDEALLY *WITH AN ANGLE* OR *SQUARED-OFF EDGES*, AS THEY SIT COMFORTABLY *IN THE CONTOURS*.

COLOUR THEORY

Colour theory plays a huge part in the application of make-up and is often something that is overlooked when choosing tones and shades. There are no rules in make-up but it's a good idea to know a little background, especially when it comes to colour correction.

You may hear a lot of jargon used relating to colour theory and so we have broken down some of the popular terminology for you.

We have also created a colour wheel in the accompanying app. The colour wheel simplifies the information that follows so don't worry if at first this seems a little confusing!

Colour theory in make-up application usually divides into mon-ochromatic and analogous looks:

Monochromatic is one colour applied and blended. The eyes, cheeks and lips are in varying tints, tones and shades. An example would be a brown smoky eye which blends into a lighter brown with a bronze blusher and a nude brown lipstick.

Analogous is a blend of two colours that sit next to each other on the colour wheel. The colours blend well with each other and are a good starting point to practise blending one colour into another. An example of this would be a blue eye shadow that blends through to a green onto a yellow-green with a yellow highlighter.

We will go into much more detail on colour choice for the various areas of the face and body in the subsequent chapters but famil-iarise yourself with the colour wheel in the meantime.

HUE

The pure colour, e.g. green, blue, and yellow.

VALUE

The lightness or darkness of a colour.

INTENSITY

The purity of the pigment. The brighter the pigment the higher the intensity.

TINT

The pure colour plus white.

TONE

The pure colour plus grey.

SHADE

The pure colour plus black.

MONOCHROMATIC

A blend of one colour using any tint, tone or shade.

ANALOGOUS

Colours next to one another on the colour wheel (a minimum of two but no more than five).

COMPLEMENTARY

Any two colours directly opposite each other on the colour wheel. Opposite colours enhance one another.

PRIMARY COLOURS

Red, yellow and blue. Cannot be created by mixing.

SECONDARY COLOURS

Orange, green and violet. Can be created by mixing two primary colours.

TERTIARY COLOURS

Created by mixing one primary colour and one secondary colour.

WARM COLOURS

Have a red, orange or yellow undertone. These colours are also called 'advancing colours'. Advancing colours appear to project towards you.

COOL COLOURS

Have a green, blue or violet undertone. These colours are also known as 'receding colours' and give a hollowed effect.

THE *SHORTER*
THE *BRUSH HAIR, THE*
MORE CONTROL...

…YOU *WILL* *HAVE* OVER *PRODUCT* PLACEMENT.

♦

★★★ *PIXI TIPS* ★★★

[TOOLS]

1

Decant your lipsticks into cases for use on shoots. Twist your lipstick all the way up and, using a knife (be careful), slice the lipstick bullet off at the base and put it to one side. Use a brush handle to scoop the remaining lipstick from its plastic base. Put the scrapings into your palette pot and replace the original lipstick. You have the colour in your kit and you still have your lipstick to use on yourself!

2

Don't press your brush too hard. The hairs will splay out and be damaged.

3

Use less product if you get stripes in your foundation. Once blended, you can apply more product if needed.

*"Beautiful make-up starts
with beautiful skin."*

—— *Shu Uemura*

SKIN

WE *BELIEVE* THE *SKIN* IS THE *MOST IMPORTANT* AREA TO *GET RIGHT*.

WE BELIEVE THE SKIN IS THE MOST IMPORTANT AREA TO GET RIGHT. YOU CAN HAVE THE MOST PERFECTLY BLENDED EYE SHADOW OR ACCURATELY PLACED EYELINER BUT IF YOUR FOUNDATION DOES NOT SIT WELL OR IS THE WRONG COLOUR IT THROWS THE WHOLE LOOK OFF.

We often get asked what foundation is best for a dry, flaky skin or what foundation will give a flawless finish. Our answer to this is you need to get right back to basics and take a closer look at your skincare routine. If it doesn't suit the needs of your skin type then the best foundation in the world will not look perfect.

SKINCARE

Skincare is very subjective. We all read articles or listen to celebrity choices but everybody is different. You need to identify your own needs and adapt your routine to suit.

If you have zero idea of your skin type, then book a consultation with a skincare advisor. You should expect the therapist to enquire about your medical history, your diet, your general health, how your skin reacts in different situations, how it feels after washing, how it feels by the end of the day and how it feels in certain seasons, as well as about allergies, your current routine and your work environment.

They will establish why your skin could be dry or oily and what you are doing in response so that they can identify how they can help you. They will usually look at your skin under a magnifying lamp.

It's important to be honest. If you drink five cans of sugary drink a day, survive on four hours sleep a night and often sleep in your make-up then confess all! They can give you the best possible advice.

If a consultation is not an option then do a little research online. Most premium brands have interactive questionnaires. There are also some amazing skincare blogs, as well as various YouTube channels (including our very own Pixiwoo), with unbiased reviews.

Yes, some skincare products can be expensive and they're not always the best. But if you spend money on an expensive pair of shoes once a month, then look at substituting that for a premium skincare product. If you work to a tight budget there are also great options available. After researching online, you can even make some products in your own kitchen!

Here is what to look out for when selecting your skincare.

FACE WIPES

We are always getting into trouble from our skincare-savvy friends about our face wipe abuse but it's something we are working on!

Don't get us wrong, face wipes do have a place but only really in an emergency. They don't give you a deep-down cleanse and are a major offender in blocking public sewage systems and filling landfill sites. Always dispose of them in the bin rather than down the toilet!

MICELLAR WATER

An alternative to the face wipe, micellar water was created in Paris for people to cleanse without having to use the harsh city water.

Relatively inexpensive, it can be purchased in smaller sizes for travelling or going to festivals. Massage it all over the face and around the eyes and remove with a cotton pad.

FACIAL WASH

We probably all began to use this in our teenage years as it's targeted at the younger market with promises of acne- or oil-reduction.

A fair number contain surfactants to ensure the cleanser foams up, giving that slightly stripped, tight feeling. Think how it feels to wash with soap – facial washes basically give the skin the same texture and can be quite drying.

They are not best for problematic or sensitive skin as they tend to strip the skin of its natural, protective oils. If your skin is naturally dry then don't even go there.

CLEANSING BALMS

Our personal choice (when we are not being lazy with a face wipe). Balms usually feel oily but don't make the skin oilier. They are often gentle enough to use over the eyes and on mascara too.

These need to be carefully removed – use warm water or a warm face cloth if they are particularly thick – otherwise they continue to work throughout the day. The oil in them will cause your make-up to break down and separate on the skin.

Using a balm cleanser has seriously amped up how our skin looks and is definitely worth the extra minute of effort it takes to use. We prefer Emma Hardie, Balance Me, Elemis and Eve Lom.

YOU *NEED TO IDENTIFY* YOUR *OWN NEEDS* AND *ADAPT YOUR ROUTINE* TO SUIT.

TONER IS *THE PERFECT POTION* FOR *DRY* OR *DEHYDRATED SKIN* AS IT HELPS *ATTRACT MOISTURE.*

TONING

Toners are the next step after cleansing and often forgotten. They help to clarify the skin, remove dead skin cells, balance the skin and prepare for new product. We once thought you toned only to ensure your cleanser was removed, but it's actually important in resurfacing and conditioning the skin.

Toner is the perfect potion for a dry or dehydrated skin as it helps attract moisture. For dry or dehydrated skin, a spritz-on toner is also a great option. These feel refreshing, moisturise and also help your foundation to blend into any dry patches. If your skin is in the combination or oily spectrum then a toner will help to balance.

Exfoliating toners are great at combatting blemishes or acne. They help to renew the skin and remove the dead skin cells that cause blockages. Stacey, who works with us at Pixiwoo, swears by exfoliating toners and has seen a huge reduction in skin breakouts after using them.

Good toner brands include Liz Earle and Clarins for a dry skin, and Biologique Recherche and Pixi Glow Tonic for a combination or oily skin.

SKIN TREATMENTS

If we are totally honest with you… this is the part of skincare that we suck at. We have a million reasons (read: excuses) why we don't indulge in exfoliators, masks and serums as often as we should. We have two children each and it's hard to make the time and we are lucky with our skin (mainly genetics) and find less is more.

Yet these extras can generally be a really positive inclusion. It's just all about finding what works for you. Exfoliating gives an instant oomph. It removes dull, dead skin and increases circulation to the upper layers, helping to bring fresh nutrients to the surface. Just don't over do it or you will be left with broken capillaries and sensitive skin.

Always choose an exfoliator that contains man-made, synthetic beads, usually made from polyethylene. Exfoliators containing natural beads are usually made from fruit kernels and can scratch the skin, although some people prefer that rough texture.

Serums are fluid treatments which are much thinner than normal moisturisers and sink into the deeper layer of the skin to target your specific skincare needs. They are often anti-ageing but also work to help with your skin type, and issues such redness, inflammation, luminosity, tissue damage and pigmentation.

Masks are a treat to brighten skin or to help soothe stressed, inflamed skin. Creamy masks are best for a dryer skin because they nourish and plump. Clay- or charcoal-based masks work well on a combination/oily skin type because they have great drawing properties. They pull up grime and bacteria, ensuring your pores are left clean and congestion-free.

MOISTURISERS/NIGHT TREATMENTS

Some moisturisers make your skin look greasy and affect your foundation. Some moisturisers cause your foundation to bobble up and roll off the face.

We have both been outed by many friends in the industry (mainly skincare queen Caroline Hirons) about our love of moisturisers containing mineral oil. We know it's a cheap option but, having insanely dry skin, it helps our make-up to sit better when filming tutorials.

Moisturisers are personal. They help to rehydrate and give your skin the protection it needs to face the day. You can also get moisturisers with sun protection factor (SPF), which save you an extra step in the morning although it's not enough protection for lying out in the sun.

Skin pigmentation increases and becomes darker with sun exposure so by using a moisturiser with an SPF you are giving your skin extra protection and preventing an increase in pigmentation or skin sensitivity.

At night, amp up your moisturiser. We love to use an oil. These are suitable for all skin types and are actually most beneficial for an oily or problematic skin type. Fight oil with oil!

When creating tutorials for our channel we use brands such as Embryolisse and Oilatum because they give a good amount of slip to our dry skin in preparation for foundation. Generally, we recommend Clarins, Elemis, Sunday Riley, Estée Lauder, or budget options such as The Body Shop, La Roche-Posay and Boots No7.

[SKIN TYPES]

It can be difficult to identify your skin type without in-depth questions in order to make informed choices. We have certain questions we always ask our clients and you should consider them in choosing products. Use this tick box exercise – add up the ticks to determine your skin type:

DRY SKIN

- [ ] Redness or sensitivity
- [ ] Dry or flaky
- [ ] Flat and lacking radiance
- [ ] Tight after washing
- [ ] Lacking plumpness and elasticity
- [ ] Make-up clings to facial areas
- [ ] Visible capillaries

OILY SKIN

- [ ] Open pores
- [ ] Breakouts
- [ ] Shiny an hour after cleansing
- [ ] Make-up moves easily or pools in areas to give a curdled appearance
- [ ] Sensitivity
- [ ] Blackheads, especially around the nose and chin
- [ ] Dullness

SENSITIVE SKIN

- [ ] Easily aggravated by products
- [ ] Red or patchy
- [ ] Dry patches
- [ ] Reacts to weather or certain foods and drink
- [ ] Dullness
- [ ] Blackheads
- [ ] Thinness or visible capillaries

COMBINATION SKIN

- [ ] Oily t-zone
- [ ] Normal cheeks or slightly dry cheeks
- [ ] Open pores on nose and chin
- [ ] Occasional breakouts in the centre of the face
- [ ] Tight after washing
- [ ] Make-up slides off the centre of your face during the day
- [ ] Shine only around forehead and nose

In addition to asking questions we also feel the skin and do a quick visual check to see if there are open pores or any pigmentation, as well as push the skin up to test for fine dehydration lines.

Skincare is something we have become better at identifying and applying but we believe a lot of it is genetic.

Our mum, Judy, has fabulous skin and so does our nan. But if you're not as lucky with your type, it just means you need to think more about what you are applying and you have to treat your skin kindly.

Look at your diet. Allergies and what you put into your body have a huge influence on your skin.

Eating a rainbow of fruit and veg is important. Leafy greens, such as spinach and kale are great antioxidants and vitamin C improves

STUDY *YOUR DIET* AND *RECOGNISE* WHEN YOUR DIET *IS HAVING* A *NEGATIVE EFFECT* ON *YOUR SKIN.*

collagen levels, so ensure you're eating plenty of fruit as well as vegetables such as sweet potato and broccoli.

Oily fish helps to give the skin a moisture boost and aids suppleness.

Drink up to two litres of still water a day.

Vitamin and fish oil supplements can help.

Study your diet and recognise when your diet is having a negative effect on your skin. Sugar is a hot contender for causing breakouts, as is caffeine and, for some people, dairy. Identify your aggressor and try to cut back but always consult your GP before making huge dietary changes.

Hormones have an absolutely massive impact on skin. At certain times of the month, the contraceptive pill and medication can affect hormones, but, again, be sure to consult your GP before making any changes.

Skin types have characteristics that you can identify.

DRY SKIN

- Often feels extremely tight after washing
- Appears matte with little or no shine
- Fine lines are more apparent
- Skin tone can look uneven
- Skin flushes easily
- Dehydrated (though we are pretty much all dehydrated due to the environment we live in)
- Flat and dull
- Sallow
- Oily and dry (oil on dry skin can be down to incorrect product choice leaving a film on the skin)

NORMAL SKIN

Generally well balanced with no dryness or oiliness, though we don't really think anyone has 'normal' skin; everyone has different elements.

COMBINATION SKIN

- Dry cheeks with an oily T-zone
- Open pores
- Can appear dull in places
- Blackheads and blemishes

Use balm cleansers to gently cleanse rather than strip the skin and acid toners that contain salicylic or glycolic acid. These help slough away dead skin to reveal a brighter complexion and help to prevent blemishes.

OILY SKIN

- Shine throughout the day
- Make-up will pool in areas or separate
- Flaky patches
- Open pores
- Blemishes

Use balm cleansers to nourish and hydrate but gently cleanse without stripping acid toners, to remove build-up of dead skin cells that block the pores and lead to blemishes.

SENSITIVE SKIN

- Redness
- Tightness
- Uneven tone
- Easily aggravated

Use a gentle non-foaming cleanser, such as a milk or balm to moisturise and calm. Use a lighter moisturiser that contains naturally healing ingredients such as aloe vera and camomile and natural oils such as neroli, rose or almond oil.

By identifying your skin type and appropriate skincare products, you will find selecting your base make-up products easier. Products will blend better, last longer on the skin and will enhance rather than mask your beautiful skin.

SKIN BREAKOUTS AND ACNE

Our clients and models often say, 'Oh, my skin is awful, I'm so spotty.' Nine out of ten times their skin has only one or two tiny, red bumps. These annoying spots normally arrive on a day when you need to look your best, but please know that everyone else is too consumed with how they look themselves to notice. We all get them.

Do wash your face with a suitable cleanser and follow a good skincare routine but remember that over-washing with harsh products can dry the skin to the extent that it compensates with more oil.

Don't pick at spots. They never dry up and heal. When you squeeze out the fluid, the bacteria spreads elsewhere and you are left with a red, pulsating spot that forms a hard scab. This is harder to conceal than the original red, soft spot.

One-off blemishes can be related to hormones, diet or stress. We both get the occasional spot at the same time each month and almost always on the chin. This screams hormones. We use a topical spot treatment to help reduce the inflammation. Don't apply strong, alcohol-based products that sting.

Our favourite products are oil treatments containing benzoyl peroxide or blemish creams containing salicylic acid. They exfoliate the skin without drying or stripping. Exfoliating toners prevent future blemishes and also speed up healing time.

Acne is a medical condition. It's not just a breakout in teenagers – although, unfortunately, there are still some GPs who dismiss acne as insignificant. Many will prescribe appropriate topical or oral medications. Be persistent and don't feel you have to put up with it.

PRODUCT RECOMMENDATIONS FOR PROBLEMATIC SKIN

Milk or balm cleansers (never foaming cleansers that strip the skin) and acid toners to eliminate dead skin cell build-up. Fight oil with oil and use a nourishing night oil on the skin.

Look for glycolic and salicylic acid and oils containing benzoyl peroxide. These reduce bacteria on the skin and moisturise, preventing skin from peeling around blemishes.

OVER-WASHING WITH *HARSH PRODUCTS* CAN *DRY THE SKIN* TO THE EXTENT THAT *IT COMPENSATES* WITH *MORE OIL*.

Think about all visible skin, not just the face. The neck and the ears are often forgotten but always give the game away when they appear a different colour in photos.

On an editorial shoot or with a bride be sure to buff a little foundation and bronzer over the ears and onto the neck if necessary.

It's usually around May that we realise we will expose more of our limbs to the world and it does actually get pretty hot in the UK.

MAC Face and Body foundation is a great water-based foundation for the arms and legs. We mix a little in with a body lotion and massage over the skin. It's transfer-proof, but it isn't water-resistant so be careful in humidity if you're wearing white!

SKIN DISORDERS AND INFECTION

Here are some of the skin conditions we have come across:

COLD SORES

Usually you'll feel the tingling on the lip before the cold sore appears. Immediately get an antiviral cream from the chemist. Cold sore patches can protect the area while it heals.

Avoid wearing make-up on the area to allow it to heal or at least decant liquid concealer onto the back of your hand and gently dab over the area. Alternatively, try dark lipstick if the sore is on the lip area. Scrape lipstick onto a palette and apply with a disposable brush. Never apply directly from the lipstick bullet.

At the cosmetic counter, always get the consultant to sanitise the lipstick or lip liner before application to prevent infection.

They will be more than happy to do this for you. Some brands have a beaker of Isopropyl alcohol for you to dunk lipstick.

CHICKEN SKIN AKA KERATOSIS PILARIS

We both suffered with this as teenagers and were regularly taunted (children can be so cruel!).

This is red/purple, bumpy, pimply skin, usually in the backs of your arms or thighs. Keratin builds up in the hair follicles, blocking them and causing rough patches of spotty skin. It's commonly found in adolescent females. Quite often you inherit chicken skin from your parents but it usually occurs in people with fair, dry skin.

Ensure your diet contains lots of Omega 3 fatty acids. These can be found in walnuts, oily fish, salmon and veg such as brussel sprouts.

Exfoliate your body two to three times a week or use exfoliating gloves in the shower. This loosens the keratin plugs and softens the skin. Slather on a body cream to keep the area soft and moisturised.

ECZEMA/DERMATITIS

We both suffered bouts of eczema as children and also had a recurrence during pregnancy – behind the knees, the crook of the arm and, weirdly, behind the ears. Some poor souls even get it on their eyelids. It causes itching and is worse during the summer months when these areas get sweaty.

One cause is lack of natural oil and stress can also play a huge part, as can dairy intolerance. Stacey at Pixiwoo had severe eczema as a child in reaction to cow's milk. In the early 1980s it was hard to get hold of alternative milk so her dad bought a goat from his mate down the pub (standard rural Norfolk) for its milk. She was cured!

These days a GP will prescribe topical emollients to keep the skin supple. Steroids are also often prescribed to reduce flare-ups but should be used as a short-term measure. Keep the skin clean, dry and well moisturised.

Avoid over-exposure to sun or wind. Wear cotton nightwear to reduce sweating.

Dermatitis is a similar condition. Tons of our hairdresser friends suffer from it due to their constant hand washing and exposure to chemicals.

Dermatitis is caused by irritants or allergic reactions. Quite often we have seen it as a result of contact with belt buckles, jean buttons, rings and metal arms of eyeglasses.

Avoiding the offending allergen or applying a layer of clear nail varnish to the backs of buttons or belt buckles can help. Steroid cream can be prescribed but a good rich lotion will help.

PSORIASIS

Psoriasis can be hereditary but can also be caused by the body over producing skin cells. The skin can become layered and resemble dry, hard scales in severe cases.

Specialist skin emulsions help but a little exposure to the sun can also be beneficial. Vitamin D from sunlight is known to reduce the inflammation and help reduce symptoms.

FOR ANY EXTRA INFORMATION OR HELP
REGARDING THESE CONDITIONS YOU CAN
CHECK OUT THE FOLLOWING WEBSITES:
www.nhs.uk
www.britishskinfoundation.org.uk
www.eczema.org
www.psoriasis-association.org.uk

THE EYES ARE THE FIRST FEATURE WE NOTICE. THEIR SHAPE, COLOUR, THE EYESHADOW COLOUR AND EYELINER FLICK. EYES ARE EXPRESSIVE AND OFTEN THE FIRST AREA TO SHOW SIGNS OF AGEING AND SUN-DAMAGE.

We were in our twenties when we began posting on YouTube and now we are in our late thirties we know there are visible changes to our eyes. We try to embrace them, just as everyone who wears make-up needs to make changes to their eye make-up over time. Frustration can occur when we try to apply the same products and techniques we used years ago. We all need to make a natural adjustment.

In this section we will help you select products, whatever your age, and also show you which textures, colours and finishes will benefit and enhance your beautiful eyes.

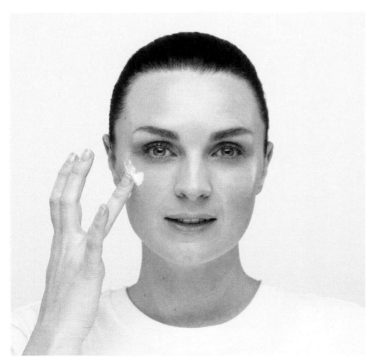

SKINCARE FOR THE EYES

The skin around the eyes is very thin and fragile, approximately 0.5mm thick. It is constantly moving as we smile or speak and is exposed to the elements daily.

Lifestyle and diet play their part and can make this area grey, dull, puffy or dehydrated. If your mother or father have dark circles then, genetically, there's a high chance you will too. Health-wise, red, irritated eyes can indicate conditions such as hayfever or food allergies.

Sunglasses are your saviour. You may feel like a bit of a diva wearing them on a dull day but they provide the best protection for the delicate eye area. Winter or summer, we always have a pair – in our handbag, in the car or balanced on our head.

Look for complete UVA/UVB protection in choosing your sunglasses. 'Fashion sunglasses' may not give you the protection you need, so be sure to check the level of block. The bigger the sunglasses, the larger the area you protect. Choose a style that sits snugly and covers the area under the eyes too.

Eye creams get mixed reviews and are quite expensive. They come in tiny pots yet promise you renewed skin around the eyes. But quite often they have similar ingredients to your regular moisturiser alongside the cooling ingredients they use to help soothe the eye area.

★★★ *TIP* ★★★
UV damage to the eyes and surrounding skin begins at an early age, so if you have young children get them some sunglasses.

If the skin around your eyes is simply dehydrated, with fine lines, then a small amount of your daily moisturiser or night treatment around the eyes is a cheaper and effective alternative.

We are rubbish at remembering to apply our skincare products and rarely get them. When we do use an eye cream we tend to go for one that illuminates. These have a light, balmy texture and are infused with super-fine, reflective particles to bounce the light off dark circles. We like to mix a little of the cream with our under-eye concealer and then apply as normal.

If it's puffiness of the skin around your eyes that concerns you then use a lightweight eye gel or an eye cream with a metal applicator ball. The metal feels cool on the skin and temporarily reduces puffiness. Using these roller balls before make-up application also helps your make-up products to sit better.

Tap on eye cream with your ring finger, which has the lightest pressure and won't drag the delicate skin. Gently pat the product around the bony socket of the eye, taking it around the brow bone and into the side of the nose. The patting motion stimulates the circulation, bringing fresh nutrients to the skin and helping to shift toxins around the eye area.

We have found cooling gel patches to be really beneficial. We love the ones made by Skyn Iceland but there are others available. These patches have a jelly-like texture and are pre-cut into a half-moon shape to fit comfortably under the eye. Infused with various cooling and calming ingredients, they will feel amazingly reviving on a stressed-out eye area.

We spend a lot of time in front of computer screens and are constantly removing and re-applying our make-up, so these are a godsend. Take ten minutes out with these on and you have an instant pick-me-up with visible results.

WE LIKE TO *MIX A LITTLE* OF THE *CREAM WITH* OUR *UNDER-EYE CONCEALER* AND THEN *APPLY* AS *NORMAL.*

YOU *CAN ALSO MAKE USE* OF YOUR HOUSEHOLD CULINARY INGREDIENTS TO CREATE *NATURAL REMEDIES.*

1

Coconut oil is great for conditioning hair and as an intensely moisturising night oil.

2

Mix oatmeal with almond oil as a body exfoliator.

3

Mash up an avocado with honey and plain yogurt to create a nourishing mask for all skin types. Slather on for ten minutes and wash off.

4

Use raw potato slices on the eyes to cool and tighten the skin. They stay cooler longer than cucumber or cooled tea bags.

DARK CIRCLES

We are often asked how to eliminate dark circles. Colour correction, foundation and concealer will help to cover the problem but you need to also look at underlying conditions:

1

Genetics (thank your parents). There isn't much you can do about this. Clever use of concealer is your best weapon.

2

Thin skin under the eye can reveal fine blood capillaries, creating a bluish tinge. Gentle under-eye massage can pep up the circulation and get the blood flowing. Use light tapping movements or pressure-point massage. Massage the under-eye area in a light, circular motion, working inwards to the nose.

3

Lack of sleep. Blood vessels under the eyes dilate when you're tired, causing a darker appearance. Reach for your cooling eye patches or eye gels. And try and get your eight hours of sleep if possible.

4

Dehydration. We always try and drink two litres of pure, still water a day. Not only will you see the results in your general appearance, but it also flushes out toxins around the eye that may be causing darkness. Water also helps with tiredness.

5

The ageing process. As we age the skin around the eyes becomes thinner and the eyes can appear more sunken. Eyelids become hooded and cast a shadow over the eye. Use eye creams as part of your skincare routine and follow our tips on applying make-up to a hooded eye.

6

Illness and medication. Unfortunately, illness often manifests itself in our skin. Certain medication can also have an effect on our circulation and healing. Try facial massage and use a light, reflective eye cream. Check with your doctor before trying anything new, as massage can be over stimulating.

EYE MAKE-UP REMOVER

We know that removing your eye make-up is the biggest chore when you're tired, but it's something you must do. It not only cleanses delicate skin around the eye but also prevents product flaking into your eye while you sleep and potentially scratching the surface.

EYE MAKE-UP WIPES

Some people use a regular face wipe but these may sting the eyes. Purpose-made eye wipes are much smaller and contain ingredients that calm and soothe the area.

BI-PHASE REMOVERS

These should be used for heavy eye make-up. One layer is oil-based and a second layer is usually water-based and has other soothing ingredients.

After a good shake, the two layers mix to create an oily substance that lifts off all even water-resistant and waterproof products. Massage this over the eyes and then remove with a cotton pad.

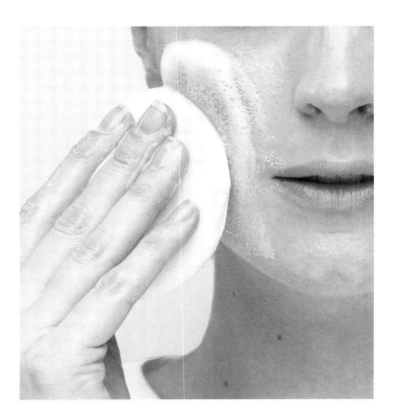

Don't use between make-up applications as it can leave an oily film and you will struggle to get products to stick to the skin afterwards.

LOTION/CREAM REMOVERS

Cream or lotion removers are great for most types of make-up. They can feel quite rich on the skin so work well on dry, dehydrated or mature skin. Massage over and remove with a cotton pad.

COTTON BUD SWABS

These are like standard cotton buds (or Q-tips) but are infused with eye make-up remover. You usually have to snap a seal to release the remover into the cotton bud. These are great both for removing eyeliner and for correcting mistakes.

SKIN *PRIMERS CREATE A BARRIER* BETWEEN THE NATURAL *OILS* AND *TEXTURE* OF *YOUR SKIN* AND *FOUNDATION.*

PRIMERS

Skin primers create a barrier between the natural oils and texture of your skin and foundation. We only wear them when we have no time to touch up our make-up or we are in a hot/humid environment.

Working on a shoot, editorial work or at a fashion week we rarely use a primer. We have to create multiple looks or adapt make-up and primer makes alterations and removal more difficult.

When doing one-off make-up application for events such as a wedding, prom or red carpet event, primers help with longevity. The finish is smoother for skin with open pores or fine lines.

Use sparingly with a duo-fibre brush or stippling brush to ensure a light application. Apply too much and you'll find your foundation bobbles up and rolls off your face.

Work primer well into the skin and leave for a minute before applying foundation. Rather than eye primers and lip primers we prefer eye pencil liner, a cream eye shadow or a lip liner.

FOUNDATIONS

It's an absolute minefield choosing a foundation and just when you think you've found the perfect one it gets discontinued. It's worth paying for a good one.

Spending £5 will get you a chalky foundation with zero longevity and odd colour options. Select texture and coverage before colour. Take into consideration your skin type and coverage needed.

FOUNDATION FOR DRY SKIN

This needs to be able to blend and provide hydration and moisture with an adaptable coverage. You need to be able to sheer the foundation over areas of patchy skin so that it doesn't cling.

A luminous or radiant finish foundation will sit well and feel comfortable. Liquid foundations have more fluidity to blend in.

Cream foundations give a great radiance and feel comfortable on the skin but cling to patches and sit in dehydration lines. Silicone-based foundations give a beautiful finish but we find the silicone clings on a dry skin.

Facial spritz is a water-based spray you can either use directly on your face or your foundation brush. It helps to blend foundation into dry areas or over patchy skin. Powder foundations are a no-no. They absorb moisture and will cake and crack.

Get wise to the ingredients in your foundation. The higher up the ingredients are listed the larger their quantity. Aqua and glycerine are good ingredients in the top five.

FOUNDATION FOR COMBINATION SKIN

Combination skin is probably the hardest foundation to suit due to the mix of textures. Cheeks are often dry so need a little moisturisation and the T-zone is oily so a matte texture is required.

You don't need a matte finish for a little skin shine. You may want radiance in areas but just matte in the centre panel of the face. To achieve this you need multiple products.

If you want a matte finish all over then a liquid foundation will be a safe option. Dust a powder over the centre of the face to absorb any oil if needed.

Powder foundation will also work on combination skin requiring a matte finish but you need the correct colour. As the powder mixes with the oils in the skin they often darken. This is called oxidisation. Combat this with primer or by opting for a slightly lighter colour than your skin tone.

You can then go in with a bronzer to warm the skin tone up. For a radiant finish use a matte primer on the T-zone and a satin finish foundation. Use a translucent powder on the T-zone and a cream or liquid highlighter on the high points of the face to add radiance.

FOUNDATION FOR OILY SKIN

The biggest problems are longevity and colour. Product pools or slips quicker and the foundation oxidises and changes colour.

Have patience and put in the prep work. Let's assume you have your perfect skincare routine in place…

Give your moisturiser a few moments to sink in. Apply an oil-free primer (silicone varieties work well on an oily skin).

Using a stippling brush (sheer cover), or a firm, chunky foundation brush (full cover), apply a small amount of liquid foundation and buff well.

Apply your concealer if required.

Leave your base for a good five minutes while you complete the rest of your make-up to allow the foundation to move and settle.

Check any areas that may need buffing in again and then powder.

Press your powder into the skin with a velour pad and then apply any bronzer, etc.

Always expect to have to touch up during the day – but at least the main base will remain.

Powder foundations will give you an instant matte finish. You can still layer with a primer first and add concealer before application.

Never keep your powder foundation sponge/pad in the compact. The oil (and bacteria) from your pad will transfer into the product causing the powder to harden and develop a film or seal.

Choosing your correct foundation shade will make or break your look. It's one of the hardest things to get right. The brands don't make it any easier to figure out.

Each company uses a different scale to grade their foundation colours. Most brands will tend to have either yellow- or pink-based foundations.

Yellow-based foundations look golden and warm in the bottle. They tend to suit more sallow skins, people who tan easily or olive skin tones.

Pink-based foundations look cooler and ashier-toned in the bottle. They suit much fairer skin tones or people who get any redness.

Quite often both undertones will suit your skin and it's just a case of deciding which you prefer.

Darker skins may need a pink base around the mouth and hairline while the rest of the face needs a yellow base.

If using two foundations is not an option then use a foundation which will suit the predominant colour and go in with a concealer in the opposite colour tone on the areas which are a different colour.

SKIN TONE CHECKLIST

- Obvious yellow or pink undertone to cleansed face
- Red undertone to chest to blend with the skin tone
- Areas requiring yellow or pink bases
- If wrist veins appear green then skin tone is warmer and requires more of a yellow base. If veins appear blue then the skin will be pink-based.
- Still confused? Swipe your closest shade in both yellow and pink onto the face and blend. The one that blends away invisibly will work best.

CHOOSING YOUR *CORRECT FOUNDATION* SHADE WILL *MAKE OR BREAK* YOUR LOOK. IT'S *ONE OF* THE *HARDEST THINGS* TO *GET RIGHT*.

FOUNDATION FOR MATURE SKIN

As the skin matures, fine and deeper set lines begin to appear and you need to be more careful in the texture of your products.

Moisturising liquid foundations, which have a soft radiant finish, are a safe bet. Look for hydrating sheer foundations or bases which contain hyaluronic acid to plump the skin. Avoid anything too heavy or cream-based that sits in lines and exaggerates them.

If you like powders, pick a very fine, pressed products, patting it into the skin well and only applying it to areas of shine.

If your skin flushes easily then try a hydrating primer which has a slight green tint. Use this sparingly under your foundation and buff in well.

A skin-calming facial spritz cools and reduces high colour. Spritz this onto your make-up brush when applying your foundation to aid blending, but also spray over the face throughout the day as needed.

CONCEALER

Cream concealers are thicker and provide a better cover. They are good for blemishes, scarring and pigmentation. Use sparingly and build up using a flat, synthetic concealer brush or a very fine, firm detail brush for smaller areas.

Liquid concealers are better around the eyes and for areas that require less cover. They are thinner so won't settle and crease as much in fine lines. Use with a fluffy blending brush to push into the skin.

Don't confuse highlighting concealer pens with regular concealers (think YSL Touche Éclat). These give radiance rather than conceal and will leave you with those classic panda eyes in photographs. Use these to add natural highlights.

COSMETIC CAMOUFLAGE

Camouflage make-up should be used to cover acne, birthmarks and other skin pigmentation, vitiligo, rosacea, chloasma and tattoos.

They provide complete cover and even skin colour while protecting the skin underneath and are usually water-resistant or waterproof. A normal concealer will not perform as well over areas that require strong coverage.

We recommended waiting six months post-surgery before applying on scars to ensure the area has healed.

Camouflage creams are dermatologically tested and suitable for all skin types. Any age can use them and they usually come in a vast colour selection. These specialist products are often only available to purchase online or in selected salons. Most brands offer a sample kit containing a selection of shades. They also include small vials of the finishing powders and colour correcting powders to set the cream. Make-up artists should keep a kit in each colour in case a job requires it.

Camouflage creams are very thick and only require a small amount of product. Ensure skin is moisturised before applying the camouflage cream directly onto the skin using a cosmetic sponge with a rolling action. You don't need much pressure if the area is sensitive.

★★★ *TIP* ★★★
Take a little of your normal foundation over the top if needed, but it may affect the water resistance of the camouflage cream.

Give the cream a good few minutes to sink in and adhere to the skin. Buff the edges with a soft blending brush. We then like to apply regular foundation to the rest of the face and buff this into the edges of the colour correction patch. Dust over the specialist powder to set the cream with a large, soft brush and pat the powder over the area rather than buffing.

For tattoos, use the colour wheel to select the opposite colour for toning down the majority colour.

To knock back the black or ashy grey-toned outlines, apply a soft peach or orange first in a small quantity. If the tattoo has a lot of green or blue then apply an orange or red first. Use a regular colour corrector if possible but a lip liner or lipstick in red or orange will work well. Buff a small amount over the tattoo and sponge on your camouflage cream.

Good brands to check out for specialist cosmetic camouflage are: Keromask, Dermablend, and Veil Cover cream.

CONCEALING BLEMISHES

Concealing blemishes is totally different to slapping on a bit of under-eye concealer and blending with your finger. You need to prep the skin, work hygienically and be precise with your colour and technique.

Blemishes are hard lumps under the skin. Unless picked or annoyed they are smooth, but red, hot and slightly raised. Nothing will make them appear flat so you just have to work on toning down the redness.

Remember hideous woodchip wallpaper? If you paint over the woodchip you will still see the knobbly, bumpy texture underneath. To get a smooth wall you need to remove the bumpy texture first. It's the same with bumps on the skin.

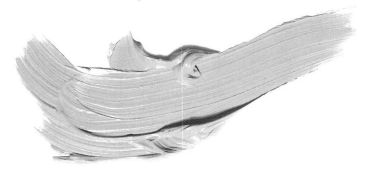

*CONCEALING **BLEMISHES** IS TOTALLY DIFFERENT TO SLAPPING ON A BIT OF UNDER-EYE CONCEALER AND BLENDING WITH YOUR FINGER.*

YOU NEED TO GET YOUR SKINCARE RIGHT BEFORE YOU INVEST IN FOUNDATION:

1
Apply foundation as normal.

2
Use a cream concealer on a firm, flat brush and push a minimal amount of the concealer onto the spot using the flat of the brush.

3
Use a clean, fluffy brush to blend the edges into the skin. Build the concealer up if necessary.

4
Leave for a few moments and then apply a small amount of loose powder on a small brush. Dab the powder on.

5
Concealing a blemish covered with dry skin or a scab needs a little more work.

6
Apply your moisturiser and blemish treatment and allow them to sink in.

7
Use a small, soft brush, such as an eye shadow blending brush, to apply your foundation over the area.

8
You can give the area a spritz with a facial water spray and use this moisture to blend the foundation.

9
Grab a cream concealer and, using a fine, firm eye lining brush, apply the concealer in tiny, delicate strokes to any areas of redness.

10
Touch up through the day if necessary. Avoid powdering a dry blemish with a scab, as the moisture in the skin will be absorbed and powder adheres to dry patches.

★★★ *TIP* ★★★

It's super-important to use a clean brush on the blemish. Clean and sanitise your brush after use.

POWDER

Powder helps to mattify the skin and set the foundation and concealer underneath but it's not a necessity.

Loose powder has a natural finish. A good powder releases a plume of fine powder when you open the lid. Control application with a small dusting brush to specific areas.

Pressed powders are great to keep in your bag for touch-ups. They tend to give a sheer to medium cover. Apply with a pad and remember to turn your pad over if storing in the palette case to avoid oil transferring into the powder and causing a seal.

Blot powders are colourless or have a small percentage of colour pigment and don't oxidise. These are great for very oily skin, removing shine but don't colour or cover.

PRESSED *POWDERS* ARE *GREAT* TO KEEP IN *YOUR BAG* FOR *TOUCH-UPS.*

COLOUR CORRECTORS

These are great for rosacea or flushing (naturally, menopausal or after alcohol/spicy food). They pep up a dull skin, tone down ashy, dark circles or neutralise a sallow skin.

Good colour correcting will create a veil over natural tones, helping them to blend in naturally. Kind of like using a photographic filter.

Use minimal amounts and blend well.

Apply liquid primer style colour corrector after moisturiser and before your foundation. Buff with a stippling brush over the areas required. Alternatively, blend a pea-sized amount with your moisturiser.

Apply cream colour corrector under your foundation or mix a little in with your regular concealer and use it on top.

Apply powder colour corrector by dusting lightly. A pink, loose powder is particularly good at toning down yellow foundation.

Use our colour wheel to choose the tone of colour corrector. Look at the colour you are trying to hide on the wheel and then look to the opposite side for the balancing colour.

For example, dark grey or purple circles under your eyes are balanced by a warm, peach- or yellow-based corrector.

USE GREEN FOR:

- Toning down red/pink blemishes
- Rosacea
- Scarring
- Skin flushing
- Allergic skin

USE ORANGE/PEACH FOR:

- Grey or purple dark circles
- Bruising
- Giving radiance to a darker skin tone
- Lifting an ashy/dull skin tone

USE YELLOW FOR:

- Brightening a pale ashy skin tone
- Use as an eye shadow base on a veiny eyelid

USE PINK FOR:

- Brightening a lighter skin tone
- Faded bruises with a green/yellow undertone
- Ashy patches on a medium skin tone

USE PURPLE OR LAVENDER FOR:

- Sallow/yellow skin tone
- Times when you have been ill and need a boost
- Evening out a patchy tan

★★★ *TIP* ★★★

For oily skin, if you prefer not to use powder at all then paper blotting sheets are great. They often come in a handy-sized packet with small sheets of highly absorbent paper to absorb oil on the face. They don't disturb your base make-up and won't leave residue.

TANNING

We are all aware of the dangers of the sun and tanning beds. Fake tans are a great alternative but we have seen some pretty obvious disasters. Orange patches on the elbows and heels, orange fuzz on the chin, streaky legs and tanned palms are the main offenders.

Most fake tans work in the same way: you apply, leave them on for a few hours and then shower off. Never apply and then go out for the evening! It's gross, it stinks, it develops throughout the night and if it rains then you're screwed. It can also stain clothes.

Salon tanning is good if you're short of time or just don't want to risk getting it wrong. It's possibly one of the most ridiculous situations you will find yourself in; naked except for a pair of see-through paper knickers and a shower cap, legs spread and arms up, all in front of a total stranger. The worst bit is when they ask you to turn around and hoist your bum cheeks up to get to the patch which is obviously covered by your sagging cheeks! It takes minutes though, and they are always super-professional and discreet.

If driving, park close to the salon and wear flip-flops to avoid marking your feet. Take a bin bag to sit on for your drive home to avoid staining your car seat. When you leave, dressed in some hideous, loose tracksuit, you can guarantee you'll bump into some-one you know. If that all sounds too traumatic then purchase your own and have a go.

GRADUAL TANNERS

These are great to start with. Just like an ordinary body lotion, you apply in the morning or evening and it will slowly give you a tint to your skin throughout the week. Control the level of tan by applying every day or every other day. Gradual liquid tanners mix with your face moisturiser to give you sun-kissed skin.

LIQUIDS

These are runny, usually tinted on application and are easily splashed onto the floor or curtains. They sneakily run down the back of your legs without you realising.

MOUSSE

Easy to handle and massage. You need to use a lot as it doesn't spread far. We find it dries quickly so apply and blend quickly.

SPRAYS

Good at getting to the hard-to-reach areas but also hard to control. Best applied standing in the shower with the door closed.

At least 24 hours before applying tan, exfoliate your body and face. Concentrate on heels, elbows and any dry skin. Slather on body lotion and really work it into the elbows and knees.

Think about where you would tan naturally: don't apply too much to the underside of the forearms or armpits. You can use a gadget which looks like a bathing loofah on a long handle to reach your back and bottom.

Select your tan and, using a tanning mitt, begin to apply to the body in sweeping, circular movements.

Apply just before you go to bed to develop while you sleep. The downside is that you never get a good night's sleep. Fake tan seems to make you sweat more.

Lay an old towel over the pillow and bed sheet and sleep in loose-fitting old clothes or under a dressing gown to avoid transfer of product. Shower off in the morning and apply lots of moisturiser.

SUN PROTECTION

For centuries, a tan was seen as something the lower classes had – those who had to be outside or plough the fields were tanned from their work. It's only since the 1920s that it became a desirable look.

Sun protection needs to be instilled from a young age. Most of the sun exposure we receive in our lifetime happens before we hit our twenties.

New regulations and changing medical advice can be confusing, so here are our tips:

Your sunscreen should protect you from both UVA and UVB rays. UVA (Ultra Violet A) rays penetrate through to the deeper layers of the skin. They damage the cells deep within. These rays tan and, unfortunately, are also linked to skin cancer and skin ageing.

UVB (Ultra Violet B) cause the agonising sunburn you see a lot of Brits sporting as soon as the sun makes an appearance.

Apply a minimum of SPF 15 (UVA/UVB). Don't be stingy. You need a lot more than you think and need to re-apply at least every two hours. Alternatively, look for brands that require just one application for up to ten hours.

For a combination or oily skin type, you should opt for a specialist facial sunscreen.

If you are not sunbathing, a primer or foundation with added SPF will often be enough.

YOUR SUNSCREEN SHOULD PROTECT YOU FROM *BOTH* UVA AND UVB RAYS.

[SKIN]

1

If you are unsure about foundation, go lighter as, generally, they warm up a little on the skin. It's easier to darken a foundation with bronzer than it is to lighten it.

2

Forgot to wash your hands after applying fake tan? Squeeze the juice of a lemon into a bowl and add in a little salt. Scrub this mixture all over your hands to help bleach out the staining naturally. This will sting if you have cuts on your hands.

3

A make-up stippling brush can stand in for a tanning mitt. Clean your brush thoroughly afterwards.

4

Mix a little of your cream or liquid highlighter with your body cream and apply to the shoulders and shins to create definition.

5

Oil from your skin can transfer onto your phone. Each time you press the phone onto your cheek you are applying a layer of bacteria back onto the skin. Give your phone a clean over each day to avoid this.

"You must never underestimate the power of the eyebrow."
————Jack Black

BROWS

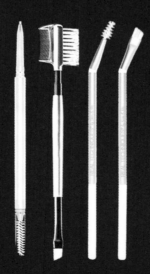

A *MINIMAL* AMOUNT
OF MAKE-UP *ON THE BROW*
CAN *MAKE* THE *BIGGEST*
DIFFERENCE, BUT
IT *CAN BE DIFFICULT*
TO *GET RIGHT*.

BROWS HAVE BECOME THE BIGGEST TREND IN MAKE-UP AND BROW-SCULPTING IS ONE OF OUR MOST REQUESTED YOUTUBE TUTORIALS.

A minimal amount of make-up on the brow can make the biggest difference, but it can be difficult to get right. Colour choice makes a huge difference although it can be tricky to get brows even.

Remember though, brows should be sisters, not twins! Making them too symmetrical can leave you looking strange.

BROW SHAPES

A good brow should complement your eye shape and blend with your hair colour. First work out where your brow should begin and end:

Hold your brush vertically so it sits at the edge of the nostril and passes through the inner corner of the eye in a straight line. This shows where your brow should begin.

Hold your brush at the edge of your nostril and angle it so that it passes through the pupil of your eye. This is the highest part of your brow arch.

To see where your brow should finish, hold the brush at the corner of the nostril and allow it to pass along the outer corner of the eye. You can apply little brow pencil dots at each of these three points to help you as you use product.

This is also a good guide to follow when shaping your brows using hair-removal methods such as tweezing. Pluck the fine hairs that fall outside the area where you hold up your brush. There really are no rules when deciding how full to wear your brows.

★★★ *TIP* ★★★
A slightly fuller brow gives a more youthful appearance.

If you are a little nervous about shaping and removing hairs, then go to a reputable salon. Get recommendations from friends whose brows you like or stop someone in the street and ask them where they go to get an immaculate brow shape. You'll make their day by asking!

If you have previously removed hair, wait around four weeks to ensure you or the therapist can grip onto the hairs easily. A good beauty therapist or brow specialist will always first ask:

What is your ideal shape? Do you have any images of brow shapes you like? How do your brow hairs fall? Are they fine or coarse hairs?

The therapist will take a close look at your brows before removing any hairs. The brow shape you have in your mind may not necessarily suit your face and a good therapist will be honest and advise you accordingly.

TWEEZING

The most obvious hair-removal method is by using tweezers. Our favourite type is slightly angled, allowing you to rest them on the skin while getting close to the root. We find angled tweezers reduce the risk of nipping your skin.

Pointed tweezers are more difficult to use because they cover a smaller surface area. They can also be a little stabby. They are good for teasing out tiny stubbly hairs or ingrown hairs. Tweezers with a squared-off end grip hairs but nip easily.

Ensure you pull hair as close to the root as possible in the direction of hair growth to avoid causing the hair follicle shape to distort. Otherwise the next hair may grow at a weird angle or become ingrown.

WAXING

We wouldn't advise doing this yourself as you can't stretch the skin and remove the wax easily on your own.

Strip wax is applied to the skin in the direction of hair growth and removed using a cloth or paper strip in the opposite direction. Strip wax is softer and has a more gloopy texture. It can be used on the brow, but it's better on larger areas of the body.

Hot wax is thicker, dries quickly and sets hard onto the hairs rather than the skin. It is usually applied against the hair growth so that it pushes the hairs up before a second layer is applied.

It's left to dry off and harden before being pulled off against the direction of hair growth. Hot wax is effective on smaller areas of the body. It can be easily controlled and doesn't require cutting up cloth strips into tiny pieces.

THREADING

Threading has been around for a long time in Asia but has become popular in the West over the last five years.

A fine piece of cotton thread is dragged along the skin in a twisting motion, trapping the hairs and pulling them out at the root. It not only removes the darker hairs but also the very fine, downy hairs that often show up under powder eye shadow. Make-up sits beautifully on a threaded brow. It's very precise and effective on problem hairs or very coarse hair. Super-quick and no more painful than tweezing hairs. It's also great for sensitive skin that reacts to chemicals.

★★★ *TIP* ★★★
Waxing is quicker and less painful than tweezing and regrowth is slower.

ELECTROLYSIS

Electrolysis is not as popular as it once was. It's a long process that can be quite costly and must be performed by a qualified therapist.

A fine needle is inserted into the hair follicle through which an electrical current is passed into the root of the hair. The root is destroyed and the hair removed using tweezers. The hair should be growing and so requires regular treatments to ensure it's zapped at the optimum time.

HD BROWS

You may have heard a lot of journalists and online gurus talking about HD Brows. We think this technique is responsible for the huge popularity of brow-shaping and probably guilty of encouraging people to become obsessive about their brow shape!

HD Brows is the brand name for a technique that basically combines all the approaches we have mentioned. An initial consultation is followed by tinting, waxing, threading, tweezing, trimming and after-care. Perfect for sculpted brows but if you prefer a more natural look we suggest sticking to your tweezers.

BROW TINTING

You may have very fine brow hairs that don't require hair removal but need tinting to add volume. We often tint our own brows using a home-dye kit before plucking. It darkens the hairs, making them easier for us to see.

It's easy to purchase a kit and do it yourself. It creates volume, you no longer need to apply cosmetic brow products, it allows you to swim without fear of your brows moving and it tints your greying or white hairs.

Apply a barrier cream, such as Vaseline, around the brow to avoid the tint staining the skin. Mix your tint up according to the instructions and, using a disposable mascara wand, gently brush the tint through the brow hairs. You can apply a thicker layer depending on the intensity. The longer you leave the tint on, the darker the colour.

Brow tinting is especially effective on red hair or silver and greying hair. However, due to the coarseness of red or grey hair you may need to leave the tint on for longer.

SEMI-PERMANENT BROW MAKE-UP

Having your brows tattooed on is the norm for some people and the number of salons offering this treatment are vast, so be sure to do your research. All good salons offer a consultation first.

The most natural semi-permanent brow is created using feathered hair strokes. It takes time and patience but in the end you will be left with a perfect brow that resembles natural hair.

A local anaesthetic is usually used to reduce sensitivity as the colour pigments are applied to the brow area using a fine needle.

This treatment will generally last from nine months to a year and a half depending on how your skin reacts with the pigment.

THERE ARE *TONS OF BROW PRODUCTS* AVAILABLE TO CREATE *DIFFERENT TEXTURES AND FINISHES*.

BROW BLEACHING

If you have naturally dark brows, it's almost impossible to make them appear lighter using traditional eyebrow make-up products. You'll just end up with some weird tone that makes your brows even more obvious. We think light hair and darker brows looks fab but we have actually done this when we've lightened our hair and felt our brows were too dark. However, our brows are very sparse so it didn't look drastically different.

Please proceed with caution. Bleaching treatments need to be applied and left on the brow hair for not much longer than one minute. They take to the hair extremely quickly.

Some hairdressers offer brow bleaching but there are also lots of good brow-bleaching products – but never use normal household bleach. If your brows are naturally dark brown or black then we would advise getting this treatment done with a hairdresser, as you run the risk of getting orange- or copper-coloured brows!

BROW PRODUCTS

There are tons of brow products available to create different textures and finishes. For the most natural finish you need to use small amounts of a few different products.

BROW PENCILS

Probably the most common type of brow product. Most brands will do brow pencils in a wide variety of shades. Pencils give a very defined one-dimensional finish to the brows and are good for filling in sparse areas or for creating shape.

Don't simply fill in your brows in a block colour. Use the pencil to create tiny, hair-like flicks. We like to use a disposable, clean mascara wand to brush through the pencil to soften the finish.

Quite often brow pencils also have a spooley-style brush to shape the hairs and soften the pencil. You should go for a pencil that feels harder and waxy. It will last longer on the skin although will require more pressure on application. A softer pencil will move in humidity and transfer easily.

BROW CREAM

These are pigmented creams with a hard texture. By creating tiny, hair-like flicks, you can build shape and colour and creams also colour the skin underneath the brow. They create a more natural texture, rather than the block finish of a pencil. We like to apply brow cream products with a very fine synthetic angled brush. Use the point of the brush to create fine hairs and the angle of the brush to draw the shape.

BROW GELS

Brow gels look like a mascara but are specifically for the brows. Tinted brow gels brush through the hairs and provide colour. You can apply gels over any other brow product. They set the brows and give texture to the hair. They catch fair hairs too, making them stand out.

BROW STAIN

Liquid brow colour applied using a felt-tip pen-style applicator. These provide a one-dimensional colour and must be used in small, hair-like strokes. These are also quick-drying – so work quickly or they will stain the skin. Brow staining is good in humidity and is long lasting but needs practice.

CHOOSING BROW COLOUR

The most important factor in achieving a beautiful, natural-looking brow. If you prefer a dramatic brow in a bold tone then feel free to skip this section!

If you have dark hair, go for a lighter colour than you think you need, to ensure they blend in and don't look blocky. If you have light brows, you need to go for a similar colour to your own hair but in a cool, ashy tone. These also work well on red hair.

Brows are never just one colour and you may need to use two shades to create a natural finish. Use a slightly darker shade on the underside of the brow and through the front of the brow and use a similar shade to your natural hair through the main body and ends of the brow. Your brows are naturally darker in these areas, so continue with this depth of tone.

Our favourite brow brand is by Anastasia Beverly Hills. They have brow powders with a lighter colour and a darker colour in one pot to allow you to mix shades.

BLONDE HAIR

Don't choose a colour that is too warm (by warm, we mean a shade with a golden or orange undertone). These don't blend and will look obvious. Go for an ashy tone with an almost greyish colour. You can always add some light strokes of an ashy brown.

It may feel alien to have any colour applied to very fair hairs, so you can use a slightly tinted, taupe brow gel. Gently brush the gel through and remove any excess with a clean brow brush.

BRUNETTE HAIR

Possibly the easiest hair colour to match, but look closely at the undertones of the hair to establish the tone. Use a lighter tone than you think you will need. This way you can build the colour to add depth. If you have a lot of red tone you can add an auburn colour.

RED HAIR

While red hair can be coarse – making brows look stiffer, thicker and even a little wavy – red brows can be extremely fair and almost non-existent.

If your hair is strawberry blonde then choose a similar tone with a caramel or honey tone. Ashy tones work really well.

For rich, auburn hair colour, go for a soft reddish-brown – almost chocolate. Your brows shouldn't be as dark or as bright as your hair colour.

BLACK HAIR

If you are lucky enough to have jet-black hair than you can go either natural or extreme. If you are not confident in filling in, avoid using a pure black brow shade as you may end up looking like an evil Disney character. Always opt for a cool-toned black and avoid reddish undertones.

GREY/SILVER HAIR

Grey hair can have a similar texture to red hair and can be quite wavy. Trim back unruly brows. A clear brow gel helps wavy hair to lay flat.

Facial features can become lost when the brow hairs turn white or silver but by applying a light taupe- or ash-coloured powder the eyes are framed and look stunning. A brow powder or pencil is best to ensure natural blending.

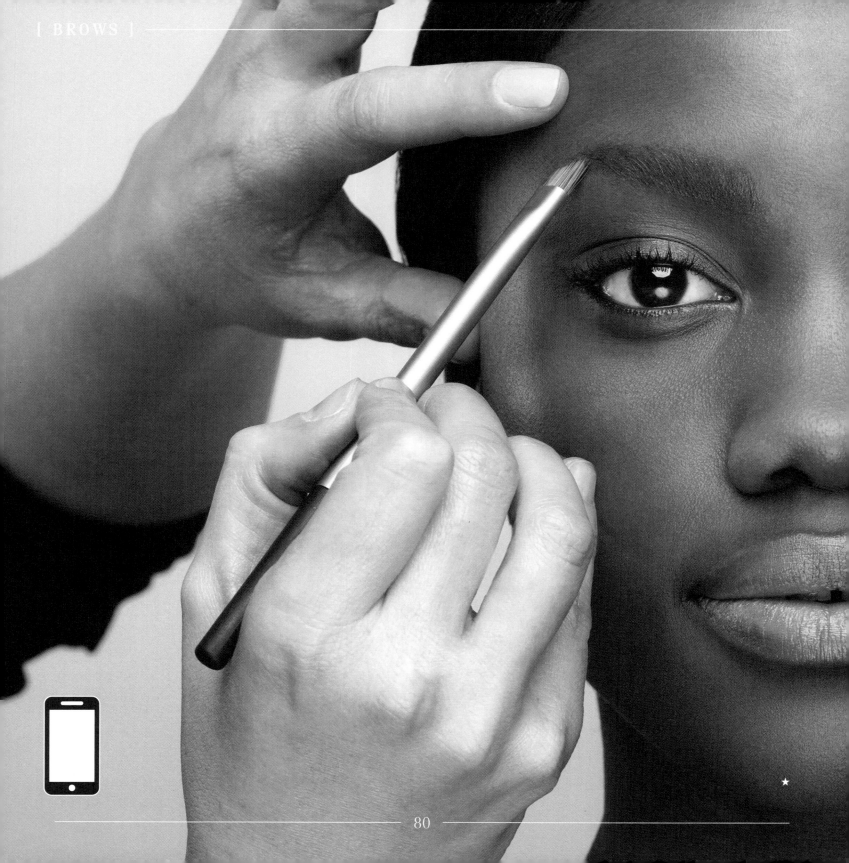

1

Be gentle, use delicate strokes and take your time.
You can use a magnifying mirror on a stand. Just be sure
to take a step back every so often.

2

Brush using a brow brush or spooley brush to see how the
hairs lie and reveal the underside shape of the brow where
you will be applying most colour.

3

In light strokes resembling hairs, begin to apply product
to the front of the brow. Don't make this area too square.

4

Apply colour to the underside of the brow,
working up to your arch.

5

Fill in the tail end of the brow. Avoid applying too much
pencil to the top and thicken with soft strokes if necessary.
Apply powder, cream or gel with a very fine angled brush.

We particularly like the Anastasia Beverly Hills No7 Brush.
Brushes should be sharply angled and slim to recreate
natural hairs. Use the shape of the angle to apply product in
fine hair-like strokes. Use the point of the brush to apply
product to the front.

6

Dampen your brush for more defined hair strokes.
Once all products are applied, brush the brows to
remove excess powder and to blend colours.

We like to finish our brows by brushing through a clear
or slightly tinted brow gel. This sets the applied colour
and also gives visible texture to the natural hairs.

7

For super-defined brows run a little concealer around the
edge of the brow. Use a small shadow brush to apply
the concealer close to the brow and using a fluffy brush,
blend the concealer. It enhances the brow angles and
takes down any skin redness.

BE *GENTLE*, USE *DELICATE* STROKES AND TAKE *YOUR TIME*.

FOR *FULLER BROWS* USE A *BROW GEL* TO *BRUSH* THE BROWS *UPWARDS.*

[BROWS]

1 Brows are sisters, not twins. One brow often sits higher due to the muscle tone underneath. Don't try to make them too symmetrical.

2 One brow may have hairs sticking up or down. This is usually the side you sleep on. Try alternating the side you sleep on or invest in a silk pillowcase that won't grip the hairs.

3 Steam your face over a bowl of hot water or hold a warm face cloth on the brows for five minutes. This opens the follicles and allows hair to be plucked with a little less pain!

4 We all have those fine, downy hairs around the brow. These pick up fake tan or foundation that has been applied to the skin, giving you a weird orange fuzz around the brow. Avoid applying foundation over the brow and blend any overlap with a small fluffy brush.

5 Train unruly brows to sit in the direction of your choice. Before bedtime, give the brows a good brushing upwards and brush through some Vaseline or castor oil. This helps hairs to lie flat and over time they will begin to behave. Castor oil is also good at helping hair growth.

*"Beauty is something you feel
inside and it reflects in your eyes.
It's not physical."*

—————— *Sophia Loren*

EYES

YOU MAY HAVE *ONE EYE* WHICH IS *A DIFFERENT SIZE* OR *SHAPE* FROM *THE OTHER* SO *IT'S IMPORTANT* TO IDENTIFY *YOUR SHAPE* SO THAT YOU CAN *BEST APPLY* PRODUCT.

EYE SHAPES

There are common shapes and each can be altered.

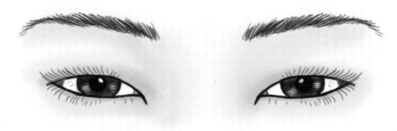

MONOLID

'Mono' translates as 'one' and a monolid is one lid. It doesn't have a socket line or a crease. When looked at in profile the lid appears flat from the eyebrow down to the lash line. It can sometimes appear a little puffy.

You will know if you have a monolid when you look directly into a mirror because you will see flat skin rather than a crease.

Find your natural eye crease or socket line by locating the socket bone right above your eyeball. The crease falls below that bony area.

You can create a crease by using a dark eyeshadow, but you need to be quite skilled at make-up application. It looks great from a distance but close up it can be quite obviously fake. A false crease sits just above the eye and needs to be blended well. Place the crease in exactly the same position on the opposite eye.

Working on make-up counters we encountered women who used eyelid tape on their monolids. These slim slithers of sticky tape, popular in the Far East, adhere to the lid and are pushed into the orbit of the eye to create a socket. The tape is usually transparent, although this can sometimes make it tricky to apply colour over

the top. They can be purchased in eyeshadow colours or in black to help them blend in when wearing full eye make-up.

Apply your eyeshadow in a block across the lash line and blend the colour upwards – darker at the lash line and lighter as it blends towards the brow. Liquid or gel liner at the lash line works well at giving definition.

HOODED EYES

Some people are born with a hooded eyelid and some develop one as they age. Either way, the upper lid falls over your natural crease. It can resemble a monolid by hiding the crease underneath the upper lid.

To see where to apply colour in your natural crease, hold a mirror low and look down into it. Any colour applied to the socket will be covered by the hooded lid.

Apply eyeshadow in the same way as you would for a monolid, with the strongest amount of colour at the lash line, blending upwards in a block. The colour should run in a gradient from dark through to light. You may need to take your eyeshadow higher towards the brow. Also try winging the eyeshadow out at the edges of the eye. This creates a feline effect and gives the eye an almost shape. Corner eyelashes at the outer edge of the eye will enhance this type of shadow application.

THE *EYES ARE*
THE *FIRST FEATURE*
WE *NOTICE.*

UPTURNED EYES

We love this shape. It's the classic almond shape and looks very youthful. Imagine there is a line running horizontally through the centre of your pupil as you look straight in a mirror. The outer corners of an upturned eye will sit higher than the imaginary line.

To balance upturned corners, keep the eyeshadow at the outer edge of the eyelid darker and blend it softly around and under the eye. Apply eyeshadow or a pencil liner along the corner of the bottom lashes. This will make the lower lash line appear even and lowered.

Use a kohl or pencil liner on the waterline of the eye, the fleshy part of the inner lower lash line, from where your lower eye lashes project. Keep the kohl to the outer edge. Apply more mascara to the bottom lashes than the top to draw attention away from the upturned corner.

DOWNTURNED EYES

Imagine a line running horizontally through the pupil. If the outer edge of the eye sits below that line then the eyes are downturned. They can seem slightly sad.

Your eyes can be lifted at the edges if you keep your darkest eyeshadow on the upper lid and blend upwards towards the corner of the brow. You can also use pencil or liquid liner along the upper lash line and create a winged flick, angled upwards.

Curling the upper lashes and applying corner false lashes will enhance and lift the outer edge.

CURLING THE *UPPER LASHES* AND APPLYING *CORNER FALSE LASHES* WILL *ENHANCE* AND *LIFT* THE *OUTER EDGE.*

★★★ *TIP* ★★★
Avoid placing too much colour underneath the eye.

ROUND EYES

You can often see the whites of round eyes around the iris and you can combat this by creating a more elongated shape. At the most rounded area of the upper eyelid, keep the darkest eyeshadow close to the lash line and blend the eyeshadow straight across towards the outer edge.

Start eyeliner at the outer corner of the iris and wing it out in a straight line rather than following the shape of the eye. Mirror the eyeshadow shape under the eye, sweeping it along in a straight line towards the outer edge.

Don't curl your eyelashes as this will enhance the centre of the eye. Apply less mascara to the middle section of the eye and give the inner and outer corner lashes a good coat of mascara. Very short, individual lashes applied to the inner and outer corner of the eye can help.

SMALL EYES

Correcting small eyes is more about eyeshadow colour. Choose lighter colours that have a light reflective finish. Using a wash of

a light-coloured, reflective eyeshadow over the lid will open the eyes. Keep darker eyeshadow to the outer edge and socket line of the eyes, creating an inverted 'C' shape at the edge. Don't apply your eyeshadow in a block all the way along the eyelid.

Avoid eyeshadow under the lower lashes. Blend a soft liner across the upper lash line and wing it out softly. Use a flesh-coloured or off-white eye pencil in the waterline of the lower eye. This will instantly brighten and whiten the eye. Give the lashes a good curl and apply lashings of mascara to both top and bottom lashes.

PROTRUDING EYES

You will never totally be able to make your protruding eye appear flat. The natural shape of your eye will always be there. But you can help by avoiding overly shimmery products or light-reflecting colours that project light and make the eyes more prominent.

Matte eyeshadow (especially darker shades) is your best weapon. Apply your shadow just as you would for round eyes, using an eye kohl in any dark shade to the waterline of the eye from the inner corner across to the outer corner.

If you are confident, apply the same pencil to the waterline of the upper eyelid also. By coating the upper and lower waterlines of the eye you will downplay the projection.

CLOSE-SET EYES

Evenly spaced eyes, in theory, would allow another eye to fit between them. If not, they are close-set, when the inner corners of each eye appear to be very close to the side of the nose, with more space at the outer corner.

Use light-coloured eyeshadow on the inner corner and blend a darker colour at the outer, drawing the outer edge more widely. You can use liner, beginning at the start of the iris of the eye and winging out to make your desired shape. Keep your mascara to the outer edge and don't apply any to the fine lashes on the inner corner.

WIDE-SET EYES

If another eye could easily fit between your eyes you can draw the eyes together. Apply eyeshadow in a block all over the eyelid and use a little bronzer through the inner corner and inner socket of your eye. This will create a natural-looking shadow on the inside of the eye.

Line the inner corners of your waterline with a kohl to give the illusion of the eyes sitting closer together.

Focus your mascara on the inner, fine lashes with a sheer application to the outer edge.

DEEP-SET EYES

You will know if you have deep-set eyes because your brow bone protrudes further than your eyeball. Strong, high cheekbones may accentuate this.

Bring the eyes forward with light eyeshadow shades. Shimmer or satin-finish eyeshadows will also help achieve a brighter, more open eyelid.

Curling the lashes and using tons of mascara draw the eyes forward. Coloured mascara also works really well, drawing attention to the eyes and brightening the area. Be sure to also keep your brow shape in check, tweezing low-lying hairs to open up the eye area.

★★★ *TIP* ★★★

You can use an eyeshadow that's a few shades darker than your natural skin tone.

EYE MAKE-UP FOR GLASSES AND CONTACT LENS WEARERS

Spectacle wearers always ask us how to use make-up to enhance their eyes and just because you wear glasses doesn't mean you have to compromise on your make-up. Application can be the hardest part – you might not be able to see what you're doing without them but you can't put it on wearing them!

Your eyes can get a little lost behind frames. Rimless glasses are great unless you need frames to support stronger prescription lenses, when you can try a lighter-coloured, ombré or thinner frame. Frames upturned in an almond shape show more of the sides of the eyes.

You can guide application with a lighted magnifying mirror on a stand, leaving your hands free to support your eyelid and apply colour. Specialist make-up eyeglasses work really well although they do look a little crazy. Each magnified lens is on a hinge and while one is flipped up you can see through the other.

Apply your eye make-up as we recommend, but perhaps try a brighter shade or go a little darker to make it stand out. Eyeliner gives the eyes definition if you don't want to wear eyeshadow. A thin application of liquid liner to the upper lashes or soft kohl pencil blended around and under the eye enhances the shape and adds definition.

Long, luscious lashes can hit glasses and bend back or feel uncomfortable when you wear mascara. Try eyelash tinting. You can still have the dark lashes without the curl.

If you wear contact lenses, remember that eyeshadow powders with glitter or a granular texture may drop down into the eye and cause irritation. Avoid them or apply your make-up before you put in your lenses and always carry a spare pair.

Some mascaras that provide volume may contain tiny nylon fibres that cling to the lashes to enhance their thickness and length. These fibres inevitably drop and cling to contact lenses and these mascaras are best avoided. You can spot them by the tiny, hair-like pieces they leave on the wand. Stick to the use-by date on all products. Ageing make-up becomes dry, flaky and harbours bacteria that can get onto the lens and cause pretty nasty eye infections.

EYE PRIMER

Primers can help with longevity and if you have oily eyelids or are in a humid country. They will contain talc that helps to absorb oil from the lid and colour to stay in place.

Primers can be applied all over the eyelid and up to the brow, providing a barrier between the skin and any cosmetic product. They help to prevent creasing and movement of your eyeshadow and aid in its blending. To combat discolouration or dullness on the lid, look for primers tinted in a peach tone or those containing light-reflective pigments.

THE *TRICK WITH EYE PRIMER* IS TO *APPLY A SMALL* AMOUNT, *BUFFED OVER* THE *EYELID* WITH A *FLUFFY BRUSH*.

★★★ TIP ★★★
Assess your eyelids throughout the day – you may not even need a primer.

Universal eye primers can be colourless or coloured for a specific tone. Very deep skin tones require a peach or golden tint. The trick with eye primer is to apply a small amount, buffed over the eyelid with a fluffy brush. A sheer veil absorbs oil and dries quickly so you can instantly apply eyeshadow without slipping on the lid and causing a crease.

CREAM EYESHADOW

We adore cream eyeshadows. They are a super-easy texture to work with, are very forgiving of mistakes and work well with powder eyeshadow to give more vibrancy.

Creams usually come in a pot or in a twist-up lipstick-style applicator. Screw the lid on tightly otherwise the cream dries and shrinks.

Cream eyeshadow can be worn on its own as a sheer wash over the eye or you can blend multiple cream colours, remembering they will merge rather than settling on the skin separately as powders do.

Some creams dry on the skin, which is great for longevity, but blend quickly to avoid a patchy finish.

Cream eyeshadows make a fantastic base for your powder eye-shadow. We actually prefer to use them as a base instead of a primer, but stick with a primer if you have oily eyelids. Cream eyeshadow evens out the eyelid and helps any powder eyeshadow you apply to adhere and appear more vibrant and bold.

Create a unique colour by applying a vibrant-coloured cream eye-shadow underneath a contrasting powder eyeshadow. Powder is a safer option on a mature lid, as creams sink into creases and enhance the skin texture over fine lines. You can use a primer to combat this but the cream usually always settles.

POWDER EYESHADOW

Powder eyeshadows are widely used as eyeshadow texture. They are either pressed into a pot or in a palette alongside comple-mentary shades.

Powder eyeshadows can be hit or miss. Some are formulated well, have good quality ingredients and are carefully pressed into the compact. Cheaper ingredients may be crumbly, smash easily in the palette and also cause 'fall -out' or 'drop-down', when powder particles drop onto the cheek (and carpet!) in application.

Some colour pigments used in eyeshadow drop more than others. In our experience, black, purple and blue powder eyeshadows are the worst offenders.

Powder eyeshadows can be divided into many categories depending on the finish and each brand has its own terminology.

★★★ TIP ★★★
The best way to apply a cream eyeshadow is using a synthetic brush, which doesn't absorb the product.

MATTE FINISH

This texture has zero shine or shimmer. It is a flat, one-dimensional colour and can be tricky to work with as it has a much dryer formula. Matte shades are notoriously hard to blend and darker matte shades can go patchy.

Matte textures create a beautiful, intense, smoky eye and are also great to use as a contour colour through the socket of the eye. They mimic the skin's natural texture. They can also be used as an eyeliner along the lash line for a softer look. On a mature eye, they sit particularly nicely as a liner because they don't move or crease.

PEARL FINISH

This is a two-tone finish that reflects differently depending on the light. They usually blend easily and have a good pay-off, by which we mean a strongly pigmented colour.

This finish works well over a cream eyeshadow, taking on the colour and texture of the cream underneath and giving off a unique colour – think of the effect of water and oil mixing on the roadside.

SATIN

This resembles the finish of satin fabric. It has a natural, even sheen with no glitter or frosting. Generally, these finishes blend really well and complement all skin types and ages.

FROSTED

Frosted shadows are infused with glitter particles. Depending on the quality, you will get a shimmering base colour that reflects the light. However, it can be difficult to get an even blend because of the sporadic glitter and particles can also drop down into the eye. It's not great for contact lens wearers and can be a problem on mature skin.

VELVET

This can have a similar finish as a satin finish, but it feels more luxurious. It sometimes has a soft light-reflective finish and can be good for blending and layering with other textures.

LOOSE-POWDER EYESHADOW

Eyeshadow powders come in a loose form so that they can be mixed with other products and used on other areas. They are often referred to as pigments by some brands. You can apply onto a clean eyelid, but they adhere better with a cream eyeshadow underneath.

Use as an eyeshadow with a firm brush, patting the colour into the eyelid. Don't blend it over with a fluffy brush which will cause the product to drop down. Loose-powder eyeshadows can also be used as blushers, but sparingly, as they are often strongly pigmented.

Light-coloured loose-powder eyeshadows such as bronze or silver can be mixed with face or body moisturiser to give skin a soft radiance. Body painters mix loose powder colours to create new, unique shades. Another fun use for them is to add colour to a clear mascara.

> EYESHADOW *POWDERS* COME IN A *LOOSE* FORM SO THAT THEY *CAN BE MIXED* WITH *OTHER PRODUCTS* AND USED ON *OTHER AREAS.*

GLITTER PIGMENTS

Like magpies, we are attracted to our little pots of loose glitter particles. Brands recommend that these are only used on the face and body – covering themselves in case you get glitter in your eye and scratch your retina! We use glitter around our eyes all the time without problems but it's down to you to decide if you want to take the (very minimal) risk.

The larger the pieces of glitter, the more likely they are to drop into the eye. Tiny, fine glitter particles won't really cause any more irritation than a frosted eyeshadow.

First coat the lid with cream eyeshadow or eye gel. Some brands sell mixing medium, a creamy film with the texture of petroleum jelly.

Using a firm brush, press the glitter onto the lid. Bits of glitter will drop down so apply your base afterwards, having first used a facial wet wipe to clear up.

Make-up artists working in studios remember that chunky shards of glitter don't photograph well. Light bounces off and reflects as a dull, grey square. Fine glitter, however, looks beautiful in the flesh and on camera, reflecting light to create a wash of shimmering colour.

★★★ *TIP* ★★★
*Be extra cautious if
you have sensitive eyes or
wear contact lenses.*

EYE COLOUR THEORY

There are no strict rules if you feel confident with contrasting colours or experimenting. The rest of us may find it useful to follow basic colour theory guidelines.

BROWN EYES

You are so lucky. Pretty much anything will go with your brown eyes, but be careful to check them, as eyes almost always contain a few flecks or tints of other colours.

Using brown colours, keep a warm, chocolate tone with a red pigment. This will enhance the richness of your eyes and create a beautiful, smoky effect.

Enhance light brown eyes with green or yellow flecks by wearing a plum- or purple-based eyeshadow. Warm taupes and any golds, from pale yellow through to warm bronzes, will also work. Olive greens can look fab with brown eyes, and navy or bright cobalt blue create a striking contrast.

BLUE EYES

Most colours will go with blue but be careful of making them appear red or sore-looking. Avoid any shades of frosty pink or red-based browns.

Orange and gold will make your blue eyes look insanely bright. Orange pigment next to blue creates a vibrant shade (think of how the sun makes the sea into a dazzling turquoise) and gold- and terracotta-toned browns work in the same way.

If you wish, you can wear blue on a blue eye but a deeper shade of blue works better. Navy or indigo work especially well.

ORANGE AND *GOLD* WILL *MAKE YOUR BLUE EYES* LOOK *INSANELY BRIGHT.*

GREEN EYES

Slate grey and black complement a green eye beautifully, as do silver and soft olive green. Apply any shade of purple to make a green eye colour pop, from lilac through to a regal purple and plum to blackberry. Cool-toned taupe and forest green will also look stunning.

GREY EYES

Black, smoky colours look great for the evening and any blue, from cornflower through to midnight blue, should work well. Warm-toned purples will make the eyes appear slightly more green or grey and neutral, soft browns sit nicely for a daytime look.

HAZEL EYES

Being a mix of brown and green you can wear the colours we have recommended for both eye colours. If your eyes have a lot of yellow tones in them use a metallic bronze.

DARK *SMOKY EYESHADOW* CAN REALLY *INTENSIFY LIGHT EYES* AND *FRAME DARK* EYES.

AS *WITH ANYTHING*, IT *TAKES TIME* AND *PATIENCE* TO CREATE A *PERFECTLY BLENDED* EYESHADOW OR A *SMOKY EYE*.

HOW TO BLEND EYESHADOW

Most importantly, you need to ensure you have the best tools for the job (also see our section on 'Tools of the Trade' p.16). If you are working with two or more eyeshadow products, you will need at least four clean brushes.

Ensure you have a fluffy blending brush to apply your base colour. This should be synthetic if you are using a cream base or natural hair if you are using a powder. You will also need at least two flat brushes to apply colour and another clean blending brush to buff the shades into each other.

Don't even attempt to use those small sponge applicators that are sold in eyeshadow palettes. They are hard to blend with, drag the delicate skin around the eye and are impossible to clean.

If using dark colours, we find it easier to complete our eye make-up before our foundation. Simply clean the drop-down with a facial wipe before you begin your base.

Here is a step-by-step guide for well-blended eyeshadow:

1

Use a colour similar to your own skin colour all over the eyelid. This will even your skin tone and create a base for the other colours. It also helps longevity. Cream base gives a more vibrant result.

2

Depending on the shape you are creating, apply your next colour with a firm, flat brush all over the moveable part of the lid up to the socket or just apply it at the outer edge and through the socket of the eye in an inverted 'C', depending on your eye shape.

3

Using a fluffy brush, blend this colour into the skin. You can apply more of the colour with a flat brush if needed but be sure to blend between each layer.

4

We like to dust our bronzer or blusher shade over the socket line of the eye. This blends edges, creates a natural contour and ties the whole look together. Use a soft, fluffy brush.

5

Use a flat brush to add highlight colours to the inner corner of the eye or under the brow bone.

6

Use a smaller flat brush to take the eyeshadow under the eye, under the lower lashes and blend well.

SIMPLE EYELINER CAN ADD DEFINITION, CREATE SHAPE OR HELP WITH ITS CORRECTION AND TURN A DAY LOOK INTO AN EVENING LOOK.

[EYELINERS]

PENCIL LINERS

A pencil will give a defined, fine line with a firm application, but remember to sharpen it with a cosmetic pencil sharpener. These are angled precisely to fit and usually contain a fine surgical blade to give an ultra fine point.

Pencils don't blend as well as an eye kohl. Great for people who don't like a smudgy, blended finish and good for a watery eye as the line holds its shape.

They last well in the waterline of the eye, but you don't want any sharp, scratchy points near your eyeball so run the pencil over the back of your hand first to soften that point.

KOHL PENCILS

Much softer than a pencil. Usually contains beeswax to help soften the product and to assist colour transfer onto the skin.

Kohls are the best option for a smudgy, soft line that blends easily and great to use in place of a cream eyeshadow. Apply as a base all over the eyelid and blend fast as they tend to dry quicker than a cream, going patchy and making it hard for you to then blend in a powder. You can also use these in the waterline of the eye but they move and wear away faster than a pencil.

FLESH-TONE PENCILS

'Flesh tone' is such a horrid name but it's the best way to describe these pencils coloured in natural skin tone shades. They are designed to be worn in the waterline of the eye, lightening its pink or red tone and creating a brighter, healthy-looking eye that looks more natural and modern than a white pencil. Light, pastel-toned liners add a flash of colour.

LIQUID LINERS

Liquid liner is notoriously hard to apply, or at least to get even on both eyes! There are different textures of liquid liner available though and some are easier to use than others.

FELT-TIP PEN-STYLE LINERS

These usually have a soft, flexible tip that applies easily. The texture is not too wet so you can build a precise shape and correct mistakes, but they dry out after three months and faster if you don't replace the cap firmly.

INKPOT-STYLE LINERS

The pots have a fine, firm application wand in the lid but the product is very wet and hard to control and better used by professionals.

The firm point creates delicate, intricate designs but drying takes longer and if you have hooded or deep-set eyes, liners will annoyingly transfer to the skin.

GEL LINERS

Our favourite and the easiest for beginners to use, although they are not sold with a brush. The gel texture is thick and easy to control. A small amount makes a strong impact and the colour pay-off is good.

Apply with a fine or angled liner brush. Dip in the brush, wipe off the excess and apply to the lash line. Begin with a light covering and build up the gel to increase depth and colour.

CAKE LINERS

These old-fashioned liners – similar to eyeshadow but with a waxier texture – are unhygienic and no longer widely used. They dry out quickly, crack and crumble apart. You have to dampen your brush or spritz a little water into the product before applying. They do remain popular in the theatre for creating strong, graphic looks that last under strong lighting.

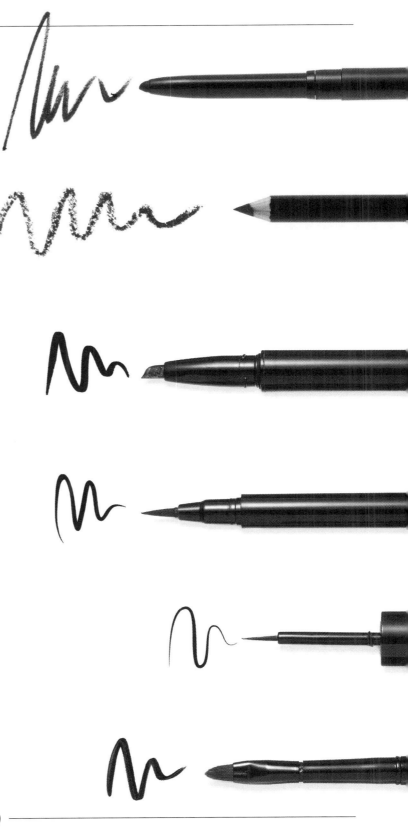

We touched on this in the eye-shape section and here is a general guide to follow for a basic liner shape:

1

Never close your eye while you apply or you may find the tail of your liner flick goes off at a weird angle. Skin is looser when the eye is open and its creases cut through the applied liner.

2

We like to have both an angled brush and a fine liner brush ready. Make sure they are clean, dry and neat.

3

Keep a few cotton buds saturated with eye make-up remover at hand to touch up or correct mistakes.

4

Position your mirror – not a hand-held – directly in front of you.

5

Using your brush or liner application wand, apply the flick of your liner at the outer edge of the eye. Apply a faint line, following the line of your bottom lash line around to the edge of your eye. You can build up and darken this later.

6

Repeat for the second eye.

7

Check your flicks. If they are uneven, remove and reapply. Better now than having to remove your whole liner later.

8

You can now close one eye and, starting from the inner corner, paint on your liner close to the lashes. With the flicks in place, you can see where to join up.

9

You should have a natural line that you can build on, darken and thicken.

You may have seen us talking about tight lining the eye. This means filling in the upper waterline that sits between your eye and the roots of your upper lashes. After applying make-up and liner you can sometimes still see pink skin under your lashes and by filling this in you will complete a much darker, smokier look.

Do this before you apply mascara. Use a soft kohl pencil. Look down into a mirror, gently pull your lid up and quickly fill in the fleshy area. Close your eye and apply a kohl liner along the lash line.

Use tape to create an extreme, winged out liner if you don't have a steady hand. Tape helps to create unique eyeshadow shapes with a defined, sharp edge.

We recommend micro-pore tape, a latex-free, hypoallergenic paper tape originally designed to hold bandages in place and available online or from chemists. It's made of paper and you can tear it to the length required. You can apply your eyeshadow or liner over the straight edge to make a sharp line.

PRACTISE, PRACTISE, PRACTISE. *THAT* IS THE *KEY* TO *SUCCESS*.

USING EMBELLISHMENTS

Sequins and gold leaf are probably not something you would use every day but they add something different for a special occasion or creating a look for an editorial or fashion week.

GOLD LEAF

Gold leaf is super fiddly and fragile but it gives an amazing finish. It's available in a book of fine golden sheets or already cut into pieces in a pot, as well as in different colours.

Gold leaf adheres to the skin but it's best to use a cream eyeshadow as a base. You can still apply powder eyeshadow on top of the cream.

After applying the rest of your make-up, simply cut the gold leaf to the desired shape or tear it into handy pieces. Using a pair of tweezers, place the leaf onto the lid and, with a firm brush, press it down onto the skin. Brush off the excess with a soft, fluffy brush.

SEQUINS AND GEMS

Online specialist make-up stores have a good variety but we often just pop down to our local craft shop and pick them up for half the price.

Dot a small amount of regular eyelash glue onto the back of the gem or sequin and tweeze it onto the skin. Apply a small amount of pressure for a few seconds to secure the gem.

To take off, use an oily eye make-up remover and gently pat over the area. After a few seconds it will lift off.

[EYES]

1

To avoid eyeshadow drop-down staining your cheeks we recommend Shadow Shields – paper segments that adhere to the under eye and project out to catch fall-out. You can purchase these online.

2

Cotton buds (or Q-tips) are a must-have for all beginners in make-up. Choose buds with one pointed tip and one paddle-shaped tip. The pointed end gets really close to the eye and under the lashes to clean up mistakes. The paddle end evens patchy areas of make-up and blends when you are on the go.

3

Loose-powder eyeshadows can also be used as blushers. Use sparingly as they are often strongly pigmented.

4

Glitter is notoriously hard to remove off your skin (and carpet and bed linen!). Our favourite tool to pick up ultra-fine glitter is micropore tape and an orange stick (a fine, wooden stick with one angled and one pointed end). Alternatively, you could use a brush handle. Wrap a piece of the micropore tape around the stick, sticky side out. Roll the stick along the skin and under the eye.

5

Buff a small amount of your concealer around the edge of the finished eye using a fluffy brush. This helps correct uneven eyeshadow shape and brightens the edge of your eye make-up.

SAM CHAPMAN

Which one beauty product would you take with you to a desert island?
Lip balm because if I'm on a desert island on my own then it doesn't really matter what I look like. I always need a lip balm for comfort and have one in every handbag.

If you could only have one item of make-up in your life, what would it be?
Mascara. It's an essential for me. I love full, voluminous lashes.

Who is your make-up icon?
I have so many. Kate Moss is my ultimate icon because she looks incredible in every style of make-up.

What's your absolute favourite make-up tip?
Match your foundation to your actual skin tone, not the colour you want your skin to appear. Dark foundations applied to pale skin look patchy and mismatched along the jawline. Light foundations on pale skin look patchy and usually ashy.

What age did you start using make-up, and how has your relationship with it changed since then?
I started using make-up (badly) at about 14 years old. I started using it to look older and now I use it to look younger. *weeps*

Whose make-up would you most like to do?
Kate Moss and Grace Jones.

Which part of the face do you like doing most?
On myself I like doing eyes but on models I love doing skin. Skin makes all the difference to the finished look.

What are your thoughts on cosmetic surgery?
I have nothing against it at all, if it makes you feel good about yourself. Just remember that nothing is permanent and the more that you have the more obvious it will look.

What are your top tips for healthy skin?
Drink water, don't smoke and use skincare and foundation suitable for your skin type.

NIC CHAPMAN

Which one beauty product would you take with you to a desert island?
Mascara, although it'd have to be waterproof if it were on a desert island! Jet black and a nice big bristly brush.

If you could only have one item of make-up in your life, what would it be?
Mascara as it opens the eyes, adds definition and is super-easy and quick to apply.

Who is your make-up icon?
Too many to mention but I especially love the era of the 1990s supermodel. Flawless skin, full brow and a nude lip. My favourite look.

What's your absolute favourite make-up tip?
Make sure your foundation matches your skin colour. A bad colour match will detract from the rest of your make-up, regardless of how well the rest is applied.

What age did you start using make-up, and how has your relationship with it changed since then?
14, I used to use make-up to hide what I looked like. Now I use it to accentuate what I look like. I like to enhance my features and work with the flaws rather than masking it all under a ton of make-up.

Whose make-up would you most like to do?
Victoria Beckham. She always looks fab but I would love to add some colour to her look.

Which part of the face do you like doing most?
Skin. It can make or break a look. Get the skin right and everything else falls into place.

What is the most common question people ask you?
How to achieve perfect skin.

What are your thoughts on cosmetic surgery?
I have no issues with it, whatever makes you feel better about yourself. I prefer when people still end up looking like themselves but each to their own.

What are your top tips for healthy skin?
Stay out of the sun and moisturise am and pm. Healthy diet and a lot of water will massively help too.

> *"At sixteen, I was a funny, skinny little thing, all eyelashes and legs. And then, suddenly people told me it was gorgeous. I thought they had gone mad."*
>
> — *Twiggy*

LASHES

CORRECTLY APPLIED *MASCARA ENHANCES* THE *APPEARANCE* OF *YOUR LASHES* AND *TRANSFORMS* THE *SHAPE* OF THE *EYE.*

YOU'RE PROBABLY WONDERING WHY LASHES HAVE THEIR OWN SECTION! BUT FOR SUCH A TINY PART OF THE FACE, THEY HAVE A HUGE IMPACT ON YOUR MAKE-UP AND HOW YOU FEEL AROUND OTHERS.

They protect the eye from dust and other floating particles, and over the years we have been enhancing them to complement our image. Correctly applied mascara enhances the appearance of your lashes and transforms the shape of the eye.

For those of us who aren't blessed with naturally long, thick lashes there are numerous products to help. The life cycle of lashes ranges from 60 to 120 days and it can feel like an age before they regrow. Lash treatments are more popular for that reason and here we'll look at the best methods for managing your lashes.

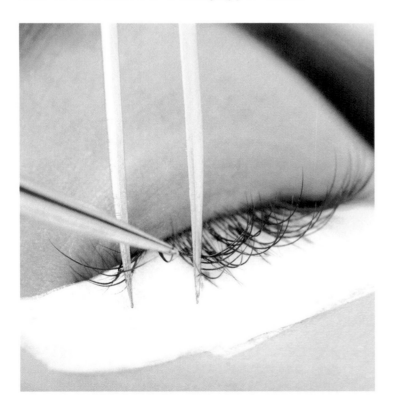

[LASH TREATMENTS]

LASH PERMING

Lash perming is less popular these days, but it's good for people who have very short or dead straight lashes and is not as laborious as getting your hair permed. It doesn't require the same harsh chemicals, but you will be lying still for 20 minutes with your eyes shut while someone fiddles about with your lashes, so it's not ideal for the claustrophobic or anxious.

A tiny roller coated in adhesive is placed at the tips of the lashes and rolled backwards to the base. A solution is applied which helps hold the curl and is removed after about 20 minutes.

The curl can look a little too extreme but it drops after a few days and you are left with nicely curled lashes without needing mascara.

LASH EXTENSIONS

Please do your research on this treatment. There are some seriously dodgy salons out there. Get recommendations from friends, research online and always go for a consultation before committing. Ask for images of their work and discuss the options available.

Extensions are usually either synthetic, silk or mink. Please do check how the mink hair is sourced at your consultation. A good salon will know the answer.

Lashes range from natural and corner only to medium and long, as well as bottom lashes. Always go one length shorter as they'll look more extreme than you think they will. Add just a few for volume or go for a full set.

False lash hairs are tiny and resemble your natural lashes. A specialist adhesive is applied to one of your natural hairs and the extension is gently applied on top. This treatment is very tedious, taking up to two hours and often salons charge you both for the treatment and then for the time on top.

Well-applied lash extensions start to drop out after about four weeks and will last around six weeks unless you have them in-filled so they don't look gappy and uneven. Occasionally, when the extension falls out it will take your natural lash with it.

Extensions offer you temporary volume and length and are perfect for a special occasion. However, make-up artists often dislike them because you can't apply mascara as its oil weakens the bonding glue and makes the lashes fall out.

LASH TINTING

Our favourite treatment and something we do regularly ourselves. Lash tinting is great if you have sparse or fair lashes, can't be bothered to wear mascara every day or will be swimming on holiday.

If you are heading to a salon rather than doing it yourself, ensure they do a patch test 24 hours before your treatment. The therapist will apply a small amount of dye to an inconspicuous area – for example, behind the ear – to ensure you don't have a allergic reaction to the tint.

Tints are available in varying shades of brown and black. The darkest colour is usually blue/black.

The tint and a solution are mixed together and applied to the lashes and is removed after around 15 minutes. Your natural lashes are a beautiful dark tone that defines the eyes without the use of mascara. This should last four to six weeks and doesn't harm your natural lashes.

LASH GROWTH SERUMS

Serums are a clear fluid applied with a fine brush. It usually contains lots of nourishing and moisturising ingredients to help strengthen and thicken your existing lashes. Though it feels like you lose lashes in the beginning, they soon grow back and seem to be much longer. We used a product called LiLash (RapidLash is also meant to be effective). Be aware, though, these are quite pricey.

We have both tried and liked humble castor oil – it's cheaper too. Available from most pharmacies, the oil is rich in omega oils, fatty acids and packed with vitamin E. It is also antibacterial and antifungal.

Apply serums by coating the base of the clean lashes in the evening. If you apply it in the morning you may find you get an oily film over the eye. Mascara doesn't sit too well on top as it separates the product.

Apply castor oil using an old mascara tube, first giving it a good clean out. Don't forget to also clean the brush. Fill the tube with the castor oil and apply to the lashes using the wand. Go over your lashes with eye make-up remover in the morning before you apply your mascara.

LASH *TINTING IS GREAT* IF YOU *HAVE SPARSE* OR *FAIR LASHES.*

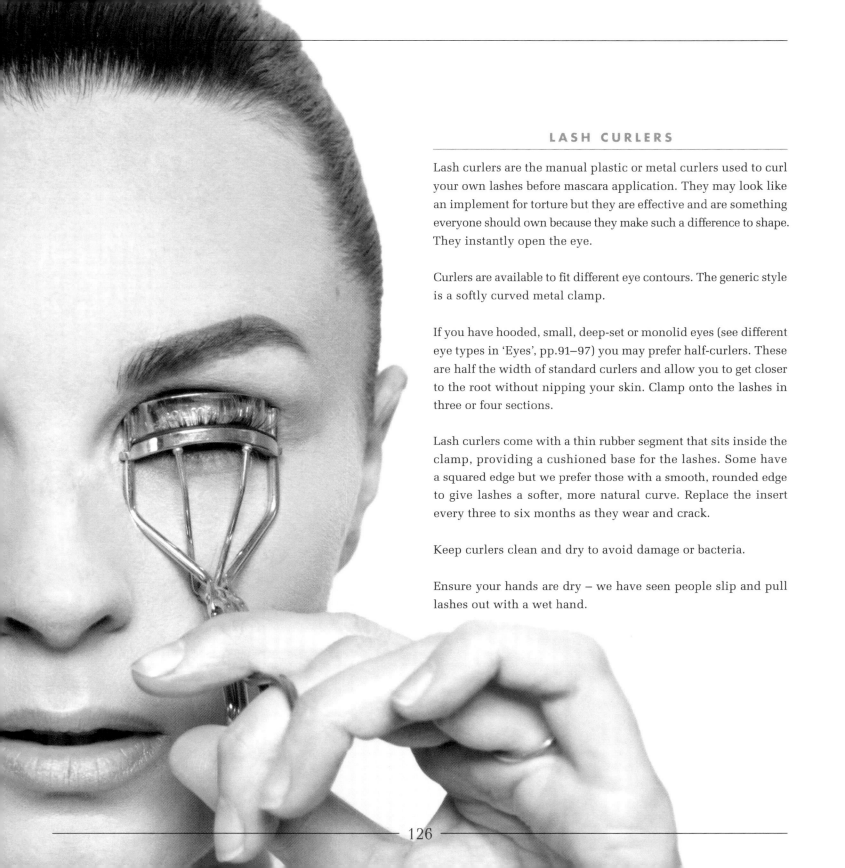

Lash curlers are the manual plastic or metal curlers used to curl your own lashes before mascara application. They may look like an implement for torture but they are effective and are something everyone should own because they make such a difference to shape. They instantly open the eye.

Curlers are available to fit different eye contours. The generic style is a softly curved metal clamp.

If you have hooded, small, deep-set or monolid eyes (see different eye types in 'Eyes', pp.91–97) you may prefer half-curlers. These are half the width of standard curlers and allow you to get closer to the root without nipping your skin. Clamp onto the lashes in three or four sections.

Lash curlers come with a thin rubber segment that sits inside the clamp, providing a cushioned base for the lashes. Some have a squared edge but we prefer those with a smooth, rounded edge to give lashes a softer, more natural curve. Replace the insert every three to six months as they wear and crack.

Keep curlers clean and dry to avoid damage or bacteria.

Ensure your hands are dry – we have seen people slip and pull lashes out with a wet hand.

We like to curl our lashes as we start our make-up, just after we apply skincare. It makes life easier: if you apply your eye shadow first you may then disturb the powder and if you catch your skin and your eye waters you will ruin your base.

Heated lash curlers are good for people who are a little scared of the traditional clamp. Heated curlers look like a long wand that you hold against the lashes and brush up to gently bend the lashes back. The heat aids the curl and holds it in place.

After curling, apply your mascara as normal.

FALSE LASHES

We love false lashes (or falsies), frequently using them in tutorials and wearing them on nights out. These days we are spoilt for choice with the different lengths, shapes, thicknesses, materials and textures available. Before you start, though, please make sure you read our section on applying false lashes (see p.130).

STRIP LASHES

These cover the width of the whole eye and are secured onto a thin band. Strip lashes are made to fit all eye shapes, so you will probably need to trim them – start from the outer corner, where the lashes are the longest so you don't alter the natural gradient.

Good quality strip lashes are usually made from real or mink hair, look soft on the eye, curve in a natural shape and blend with your natural lashes. Check that mink hair is sourced ethically. Synthetic lashes usually have a harder texture with a shiny finish.

Look closely at lashes before you buy them. Natural lashes should have finer hairs and be evenly spaced. Some have hairs that are longer or bunched together in certain areas, where they will draw attention. Consider your eye shape when deciding where the lash emphasis should be. Always go more natural than you think you want. False lashes look longer and more dramatic on the eye than in the packet.

You apply adhesive to the band, the strip from which the hairs protrude. The band's thickness depends on the length and weight of hair. Thicker bands are less flexible and are harder to apply and feel more uncomfortable. A natural band is more comfortable and also blends into the lash line easily.

INDIVIDUAL LASHES

These look like an individual hair attached to a root bulb. Often there are three or four hairs attached to one bulb. You will usually get a row of short, medium and long lashes. In our experience, the long ones are best kept for creating an avant-garde look.

Apply adhesive to the bulb and slot between your natural lashes to fill gaps and create volume where needed. They are quite fiddly but give the best finish if you prefer a natural look. Shorter lashes are good anywhere, including on the bottom lash line, but keep medium and longer lashes for the outer corners.

We advise all our brides to wear this style of lashes on their wedding day. They feel comfortable, look great and are totally undetectable – if the bride cries and one falls off it's not the end of the world.

CORNER LASHES

These are half or three-quarters of the length of standard strip lashes. The inner lashes are medium length and gradually lengthen to the outer edge. They give a feline look and create length at the eye's edge.

★★★ TIP ★★★

Applying a little black liner along the lash line also helps to blend in the false lash band.

They feel comfortable on the eye and look beautiful with a flick of black liquid liner. Position these towards the outer corner of the eye and ensure you apply lots of mascara to the centre of the eye to blend in your natural lashes.

LASH ADHESIVE

Some lashes have a sticky band and are ready to be applied straight away, while others are sold with lash glue.

This tends to get thick and gloopy so we advise buying a separate tube of lash adhesive. We love Duo, which has an easily controlled texture and dries clear.

It won't show up any little mistakes. It also comes in a darker colour and in a latex-free option.

APPLYING FALSE LASHES

We prefer to apply our mascara before our lashes to make sure we don't pull at the false lashes later and dislodge them.

In addition, once you have applied your false lashes you can't reach the natural roots so easily. Avoid mascara on false lashes, which looks more obviously fake and synthetic, unless it helps with blending.

1

Apply a small blob of glue to the back of your cleansed hand.

2

Gently drag the band of the lash through the glue.

3

Ensure the band has an even but thin covering.

4

Wave the lash for around 30 seconds so that the glue dries slightly to stop it slipping and sliding over your eyelid or sticking your lashes together.

5

Looking down into a mirror, position the centre of your lashes and push each corner down.

6

The lashes should sit on the skin at the point where your natural lashes project. Adjust them slightly if needed and then push them in sections into the skin.

REMOVING FALSE LASHES

1

To remove, first saturate a cotton pad with an oil-based eye make-up remover.

2

Hold the pad over the base of the lashes for a few seconds and then gently pull the lashes away from the skin.

3

Clean any residue off the falsies and pick away the dried glue.

4

You can usually use a pair three times before they start to lose their shape.

WE *LOVE* FALSE LASHES
(OR FALSIES), FREQUENTLY
USING THEM *IN TUTORIALS*
AND *WEARING THEM* ON
NIGHTS OUT.

LASH PRIMER

We don't bother too much with lash primer as it can make lashes look quite spikey and we prefer a softer-looking finish. Generally, it's good for sparse lashes, helping to create spidery lashes without needing to use as much mascara. Primers are white, black or clear and applied as you would mascara. Use primer to move and shape your lashes. It gives good separation.

MASCARA

Anyone can wear mascara without needing tools or being overly skilled. It takes no time to apply and is an instant pick-me-up.

Some brands seem to launch what they claim is a new, innovative mascara every month but, to be honest, while brushes and a few ingredients change they are all pretty similar. Different brush heads suit different eye shapes and growth of lashes:

SYNTHETIC MASCARA WANDS

These have plastic-looking brush heads. The bristles look quite spikey, feel firm and are slightly less flexible. The brush is usually slim. Good for people who need definition and lash separation and have fine, short or sparse lashes.

COMPACT, NATURAL BRISTLE WANDS

These have lots of fine bristles tightly packed onto the wand and are usually chunky and large. The larger barrel of the brush means the lashes curl around and have a greater bend, looking less defined but much fuller.

Product transfers easily, making it difficult to apply to smaller, close-set or hooded eyes. Good for long lashes and large eyes.

ANYONE CAN WEAR MASCARA WITHOUT NEEDING TOOLS OR BEING OVERLY SKILLED. IT TAKES NO TIME TO APPLY AND IS AN INSTANT PICK-ME-UP.

TAPERED WANDS

These have a triangle-shaped brush head ending in a small point. Greater space between bristles means more definition and volume. The tapered point catches fine lashes at the inner corner of the eyes and the bottom lashes. Use the end of the wand to pick these individual hairs out.

BOTTOM LASH MASCARA

These mini-brushes are also super slim so that you can coat the bottom lashes with ease without product transfer. They take forever to achieve a good coating on top lashes.

FIBRE MASCARA

Tiny nylon fibres, applied via the brush wand, act like extensions by clinging to the lashes and create length and volume. They drop easily if you rub your eye and we don't advise using them if you have sensitive eyes or contact lenses.

WATERPROOF MASCARA

This comes with all styles of brush head but we don't often wear it because it's such a pain to remove. Good for watery eyes, living in a humid country or if you are likely to cry.

COLOURED MASCARA

Popular back in the 1980s, it's making a comeback. Everyone's mum (and maybe dad) owned an electric blue mascara! We can thank Debbie Harry and Princess Diana for that. It can really enhance the eyes and doesn't always have to look dramatic.

You can apply from root to tip of the lash, but for a subtle finish try adding a complementary colour to the tips. We enjoy wearing coloured mascara on the bottom lashes in a vibrant colour during the summer to add something special to a natural look.

Apply straight onto bare lashes or on top of a black mascara to soften the look. For intense, vibrant lashes, paint on a white mascara, leave to dry and then cover with colour.

LASH LOSS

Lashes naturally fall out and then regrow (usually in a six-to-eight week cycle), although certain medication, disorders or alopecia can also induce loss. If your lash loss is a result of medication, stay positive and know that they will grow back, usually longer and thicker than ever!

Certain types of alopecia mean that they will not grow any longer but there are ways to create an illusion of lashes.

Smudge a soft kohl pencil along the lash line in the colour of your choice to define the eyes and give the impression of lash darkness. Keep strip lashes fine and light to be natural.

Individual lashes work particularly well on the lower lash line. Use your kohl pencil to tight line the upper waterline by applying kohl to the fleshy part of the eye where the lashes project from on the upper lid (see liner section on page 110).

[LASHES]

1 Don't pump your mascara wand in the tube. It pushes in both bacteria and air, and can cause mascara to dry out.

2 For extremely fair or red eyelashes, use a fine liner brush dipped into your mascara to paint product at the roots of lashes.

3 Always follow the use-by date on your mascara to avoid eye infections.

4 Brush your lashes through with a lash comb after applying mascara to reduce clogging and help to separate the lashes.

5 Plum-coloured mascaras enhance green and blue eyes. Green or blue mascara looks amazing on brown eyes.

6 Use an oil-based remover to take off waterproof mascara. It breaks down the product to make removal easier.

7 Always use a disposable mascara wand when working on others. Use a fresh wand for each eye and never double dip; you'll contaminate the product if your model has any eye infections.

8 Mascara on top of false lashes can look over done. Apply mascara to individual lashes before sticking them down to avoid pulling them off.

*"The most beautiful make-up of a woman is passion.
But cosmetics are easier to buy."*

———————— *Yves Saint-Laurent*

FINISHES

WE *OFTEN FEEL* THAT OUR *MAKE-UP* DOESN'T *COME TOGETHER* UNTIL WE HAVE A *TOUCH OF BRONZER* OR *BLUSHER* TO MAKE US *LOOK ALIVE* AGAIN!

FINISHERS PULL YOUR WHOLE LOOK TOGETHER. POWDER DUSTED ONTO THE SKIN. BLUSHERS AND CONTOURING PRODUCTS FIT INTO THIS CATEGORY. WE OFTEN FEEL THAT OUR MAKE-UP DOESN'T COME TOGETHER UNTIL WE HAVE A TOUCH OF BRONZER OR BLUSHER TO MAKE US LOOK ALIVE AGAIN!

FACE POWDER

Powder has been around for thousands of years. In ancient Egypt, women would use clay-based yellow ochre powder to give their face a matte but golden appearance. Japanese geishas combined rice powder and water to create the thick, white paste for that blanked-out white face. And archaeological digs continue to unearth ancient, ornate powder compacts used by wealthy women and men.

There is now so much choice in powder types that it's hard to know where to begin. But while considered a must-have, it's often over-used or even completely unnecessary. Powder can enhance your skin, but it can also make your make-up noticeably heavy and highlight skin texture.

MAKE *SURE* YOU *ARE USING* THE *RIGHT SKINCARE* FOR *YOUR SKIN TYPE.*

WHEN TO USE POWDER

If you have dry skin, note that powder absorbs moisture, but can help with base make-up longevity. Use very fine and loose powder – it releases a delicate plume of smoke-like particles when you open the container.

Use a large powder brush, lightly dusting the product. Applying too much will dry the skin and give you a duller finish. Powders with a radiant finish sit more comfortably on dry skin. Avoid applying over extremely dry skin and where there are fine or dehydration lines.

Powder is most beneficial on a combination or oily skin. It mattes the skin, absorbs excess oil and controls make-up movement.

Apply sparingly and be cautious with your colour choice, otherwise your skin ends up caked in powder that looks congealed and makes you feel you need to give your face a wash!

We receive lots of emails from people saying their powder looks almost curdled. Some powders contain too much talc or you may be over-applying.

Make sure you are using the right skincare for your skin type. Avoid foundation and concealer that is too moisturising and creamy. You can't eliminate oil entirely (and at least you won't wrinkle) but do apply thin layers of skincare, primer and foundation, with a sheer veil of powder to keep it all in place.

Use translucent (colourless) powder or select a powder a shade lighter than your natural skin tone. When powder mixes with the natural oils in your skin it oxidises and becomes slightly deeper throughout the day. It may give you an orange, patchy base... not a good look.

LOOSE POWDER

We prefer loose powder over pressed simply because we both have dry skin and don't like too much cover or oil absorption. The pots are not very portable but look beautiful on your dressing table.

It's easy and hygienic to use loose powder with a large brush and dust over the skin but use a smaller setting brush for controlled use over a smaller, specific area or to avoid transfer to contact lenses. Use matte finish for oily skin or the fine pearl finish for dryer or dull skin. The powder reduces shine and prolongs your base make-up.

PRESSED POWDER

Pressed powder comes in a compact with a mirrored lid and powder puff. These are portable but not indestructible so do keep them in a protective make-up bag.

Pressed powders, applied with a powder puff or sponge, give a slightly fuller coverage than loose powders. A medium powder brush gives a sheer wash.

Don't store pads in your compact or at least make sure the surface faces the lid, otherwise oil from your skin sinks into the powder, forming a hard film. Its bacteria will reduce the product's life and can lead to skin breakouts. Gently scrape off any film using the handle of your brush.

Translucent or coloured pressed powder varieties absorb oil, remove shine and are great for a combination skin type. Colourless blotting powder is good for particularly oily skin, providing a very sheer covering. It doesn't oxidise on the oil, change colour or curdle when layered throughout the day.

BRIGHTENING POWDER

Available in loose or pressed formula and usually infused with very delicate, light-reflecting particles. These can be ultra fine for a natural radiance or slightly chunky for a more extreme highlight. A lilac undertone will reduce yellowing and even out sallow-looking skin. Peach-based brightening powders lift a dull skin and balance ashy or grey undertones.

MINERAL POWDER

Natural ingredients have become steadily more attractive since brands began listing their ingredients on products. You can now get a mineral-based product for all areas of the face.

Iron oxides, titanium dioxide and zinc oxide are most frequently used, ground down to a very finely milled particle to form the powders' basis. Certain ingredients such as fragrance and preservatives are left out to prevent skin irritation.

We don't believe mineral products particularly help with acne, breakouts or sensitive skin but they shouldn't make the situation worse. Some brands claim they are so natural you could sleep in them but we would never recommend it.

Mineral powders feel lightweight and look sheer on the skin but the pigment, in our opinion, is never as strong or intense in colour as regular make-up.

The titanium and iron oxides often create a fine shimmer which isn't so good if you prefer a matte finish. They also flash back on camera, so avoid on your wedding day.

BRONZING

This can be dangerous in the wrong hands!

Think tactically – where would you naturally catch the sun? Chances are it would be the sides of the forehead, the bridge of the nose and across the top of the cheeks, the tops of the ears and maybe a little over the decollete. This is where you should apply bronzer.

If you have fair skin, choose a bronzer in a natural beige. Don't go more than one or two shades darker than your natural skin tone and avoid anything too warm or orange-based. The darker your skin, the darker you can go.

Test in natural light before you purchase. Ask the retail artist to apply the bronzer and then step outside. Use a large powder brush for a sheer, natural finish. For cream bronzer, use a large, synthetic-tipped stippling brush in small, circular motions.

Pressed compact bronzers are easier to apply than loose powder. Cream bronzers provide the least mess. Bronzing pearls are a little old school and messy but they do give you a mixed blend of colours.

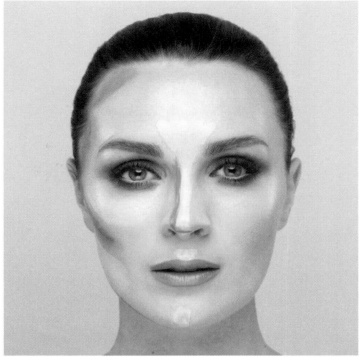

CONTOURING

Applying powder or cream of a darker shade than your natural skin tone casts a shadow, making your face seem more structured and highlighting product is then applied to the high points of the face. A darker colour generally recedes an area while highlights enhance.

The overall effect subtly alters your features but you need to be realistic: it can't change your nose or give you Angelina Jolie's pout. It's best to use a gentle contour to emphasise your naturally beautiful features.

Contouring has been the biggest story in make-up over the last five years, but we think it's had its day.

Who decided that a structured cheekbone and an elongated nose was the perfect shape face anyway? Extreme contouring belongs on the stage or under bright lights in an editorial shoot.

CONTOUR PRODUCTS

Powders give a stronger contour, but we prefer creams as they can be blended to look more natural, are easier to use and, if you make a mistake, you can just buff the product off. We also prefer to use a cream highlighter as it gives a glossy radiance that never looks caked.

A light touch and the correct colour choice are essential. Don't go for a tan or deep brown contour colour but select a shade slightly deeper than your natural skin colour with a cool, grey undertone. Sounds bizarre? These colours are present in a shadow and are

★★★ *TIP* ★★★
Strong, obvious contour never works well in daylight on the high street.

more realistic. Alternate between the application brush and a clean brush until you achieve a good blend. The correct brush selection makes a huge difference. These are our favourites:

1

Flat contour brush. Shaped like a letterbox in that they are long, slim and rectangular and used with powder products. Good for contouring large areas, such as the cheekbones, forehead or jawline. Place underneath the bone of the face and softly buff back and forth.

2

Thin, synthetic foundation brush. Pointed tip, great for cream products. Use the tip of the brush to apply your cream underneath the facial bones.

3

Angled, natural-hair brush. Bristles cut at an angled, soft gradient. Apply initial contour product, then use the angle to buff the powder into the skin and blend any hard edges.

4

Small, domed powder brush. For precision application of highlighter to high points of the face.

A *LIGHT TOUCH* AND *THE CORRECT COLOUR* CHOICE ARE *ESSENTIAL.*

SKIN BAKING

This is a technique drag queens have used for decades but we would avoid it. While great under strong lighting it looks caked and shows up any fine lines or dryness around the eyes in daylight.

You create an intense highlight by applying a thick layer of light-coloured powder on the high points of the face and under the eyes. The warmth of the skin and the barrier created by the powder heats the foundation and helps it to set. Leave the powder for up to ten minutes to 'bake' or cook the foundation underneath. It also creates a lightened area of skin that is flawlessly covered.

STROBING

This new technique is a fresh approach to contouring and hard to get wrong. All you need are your illuminating products: cream highlighters, shimmering pearl liquids or light-reflecting powders.

After applying your normal base make-up, simply apply your highlighter to the high points of the face. Imagine a light bulb above your head, bathing all the higher areas of the face in light. This is where you need to apply your highlighter. You will push back the natural contours of your face without needing a dark contour and your skin will look radiant and healthy.

Don't overdo it, as you may look a bit sweaty. Before a night out, take a test photograph of your face with the flash on. If the highlighter reflects back too much, your face will look like a disco ball so, as always, use small amounts and build up!

BLUSHER

Blusher is a product we usually apply last. It can transform a look, waking up the skin colour that has been blanked out by the base make-up.

Blusher should enhance your make-up and give your cheeks a flush of colour. We like to run a small amount through the socket of the eye to tie it all together nicely. First gently pinch your cheeks to make them flush before dusting on a little blusher. When the flush subsides you will have soft colour in the most natural position.

Just like eyeshadows, blushers come in a variety of finishes:

MATTE BLUSHERS

These are the most natural, without shimmer or shine. They usually have a strong pigment, but can sometimes go a little patchy. Use a small amount and build up.

Matte blushers apply more easily over the top of powder as they cling to moisture. If you are using one over a creamy foundation, dust a little loose powder over the cheeks first to give you a base.

SATIN BLUSHERS

These have a silky texture and may give your skin a very natural reflection. Think of how a piece of satin fabric reflects the light. Suitable for all skin types and really easy to apply and blend.

SHIMMER BLUSHERS

This either has a fine, shimmering pigment to give a glow to the cheeks or contains chunky pieces of glitter. The larger the glitter, the more extreme the light reflection and the more metallic the look. Apply sparingly.

CREAM BLUSHERS

Apply to the apples of the cheeks for a sheer, rosy flush using a small, synthetic, duo-fibre brush in a circular motion. Alternatively, use your fingertips. Pat on the colour and the warmth of your fingers will blend the blusher. Apply a tiny amount and build up.

It sits well on dry, normal or mature skin, but may slip quickly on oily skin. It'll wear off really fast if you frequently touch your face.

LIQUID BLUSHERS

Not so common, liquid blusher often comes with a small application brush in the lid. Dot on the liquid and give it a good blend with your finger or a synthetic brush. Work fast as liquid blusher dries super fast and temporarily stains the skin.

SETTING SPRAY

A setting spray is a fine mist that you can spritz over your completed make-up to help keep it in place. Use this rather than hairspray, that turns into a sticky film and can sting like crazy if you have sensitive or blemished skin. It's also not good for you to breathe in hairspray fumes or douse your face in the alcohol-laden spritz.

Most setting sprays are water-based and freshen the skin as you apply. They are also really useful to carry in case you find your foundation settles into fine lines or cakes during the day. Spritz over and re-buff your base for an instant refresh. We sometimes like to spray them onto our foundation brush to help blend our base product into the skin. They sheer out the foundation and prevent patchiness.

Setting sprays create a sheer veil and contain beneficial ingredients such as aloe and plant extracts. They form a fine barrier between your skin and the environment and also help prevent make-up transfer. If you have oily skin they will prolong your make-up's life as long as you are using the correct skincare and foundation. You also need to layer products in small amounts and remember all make-up is temporary as your skin sweats and moves.

[FINISHES]

1
When it comes to powder, less is more.

2
Avoid applying powder over fine lines. It will enhance them and actually make them appear deeper.

3
Brush through your brows and lashes after applying powder to ensure no powder residue is caught in the hairs.

4
Use a powder to correct the look of your make-up if you feel that your base is a little too yellow. Dust a pink-based powder over the skin to knock back the sallow finish of your base. The pink also helps to brighten the skin colour.

5
Loose powder in a pot is easier to keep hygienic. Dispense the correct amount with the shaker-style lid. Make sure your powder brush is clean before dipping it into the pot. Remove the powder puff from the compact to keep your pressed powder hygienically.

6
Sanitising sprays are safe to spritz over all make-up, including powder products, but don't saturate. A gentle spritz from a distance is enough to kill the bacteria.

7
Contour by the window if you're preparing for the day or in a well-lit mirror for the evening.

"Pour yourself a drink, put on some lipstick and pull yourself together."

—— *Elizabeth Taylor*

LIPS

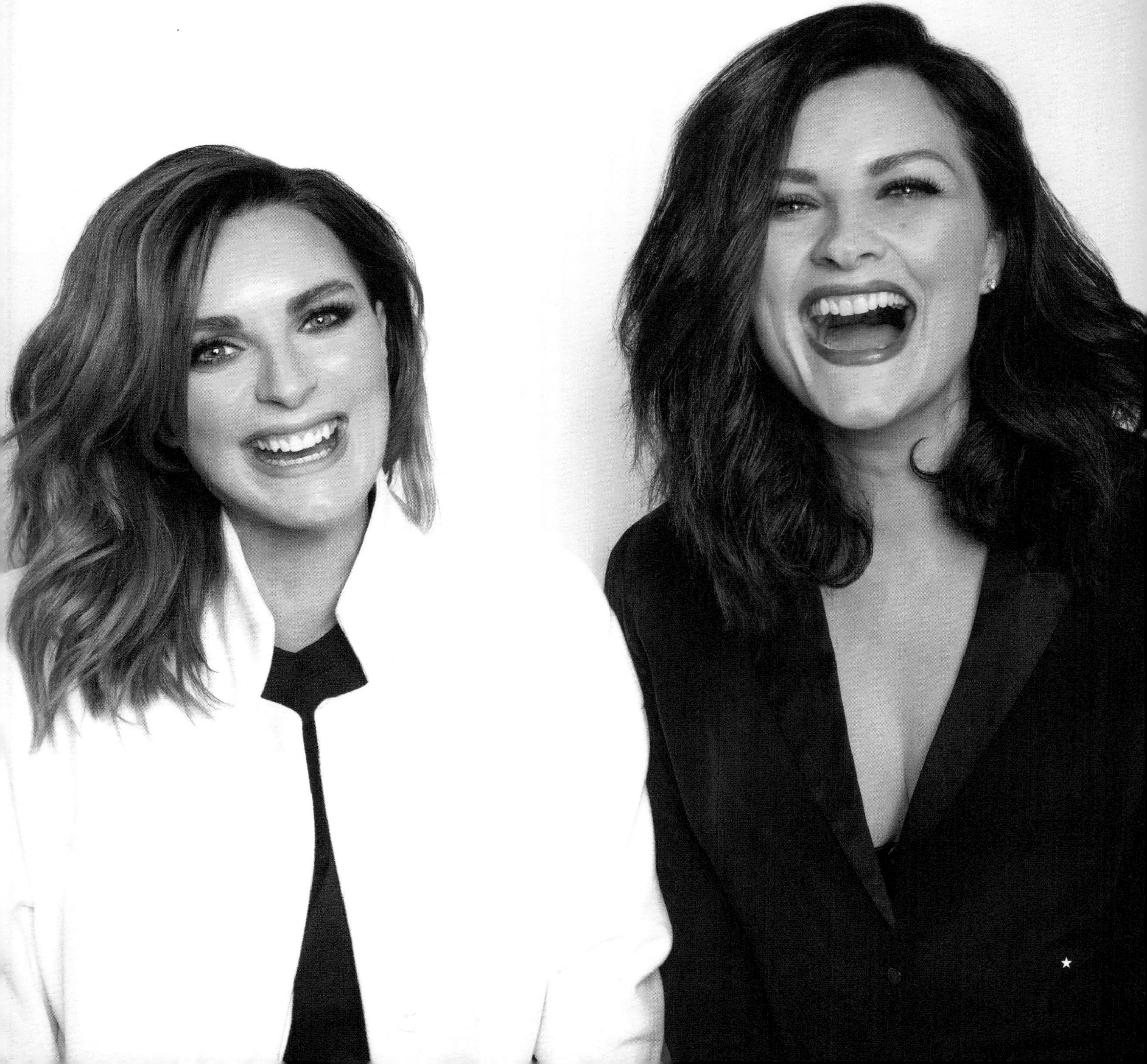

A *GREAT* LIPSTICK CAN *TOTALLY* TRANSFORM HOW YOU *LOOK* AND *FEEL*.

A GREAT LIPSTICK CAN TOTALLY TRANSFORM HOW YOU LOOK AND FEEL. IT CAN HELP TO BRIGHTEN THE FACE, CORRECT THE LIP SHAPE AND COMPLEMENT YOUR WARDROBE.

A lipstick colour can represent a whole era or allow us to recognise a certain genre or idol. It's not just colour though; the way in which a shade is applied can also nod to or trigger images of a period in time.

It's one of the only products that suits everyone, regardless of age and lip shape, and the sheer volume of shades available means that there really is something for every wearer.

Unfortunately, lips suffer in extremes of temperature and air conditioning, which means that, as you would take care of your skin, you need to look after those lips too.

Dry lips are often caused by the weather and your environment. There can be other factors such as dehydration, pregnancy or illnesses like common colds that will dry out lips.

LIP CARE

Lips are unique and unlike the rest of your skin, in that they have no sebaceous glands to help lubricate the skin and also struggle to retain moisture. This is even more reason to take good care of them.

Lip scrubs are a great product to remedy flaky, dry skin. Never use these on broken skin as they will irritate the lips further and sting. General dry patches, however, can be exfoliated away easily.

Also, natural conditioning ingredients such as olive oil, jojoba oil and honey will provide the slip on the skin and help to nourish.

The best protection for sensitive or dry lips is a good lip balm. Many balms on the market tend to have a petroleum jelly base, around which there is a lot of scaremongering and negativity in the cosmetics world.

Some say it suffocates the skin rather than moisturising it, making your lips feel dehydrated. Be sure to investigate the ingredients and select a lip balm which suits you best. Opt for a balm that has a base of plant or nut oils (unless you have a nut allergy).

LIP PRIMERS

Lip primers are never really a product we invest in. We personally feel you can adopt other methods to help with the longevity of your lip make-up. Layering a lipstick over a lip liner is just as effective.

If a lip primer interests you, make sure you apply to dry lips and after 30 seconds you can begin to apply your other lip products on top.

★★★ *TIP* ★★★
We like to apply our lip balm as part of our normal skincare routine so that the lips are prepped ready for lip colour application.

LIP *LINERS ARE NOT ESSENTIAL* FOR *EVERYDAY USE*. HOWEVER, *THEY DO HELP* WITH *LIPSTICK LONGEVITY*.

LIP LINERS

Lip liners are not essential for everyday use; however, they do help with lipstick longevity. They come in many forms: wax-based, pencils, retractable, jumbo and waterproof, and pretty much all do the same thing. Generally, the waxy, silicone-feeling liners will be the ones that perform better under humid or wet conditions. Pencil liners can feel hard and a little scratchy on the lip but they tend to have a finer point so will give you a more precise finish.

Liners are a great barrier product and a product we reach for before we opt for a primer. They help prevent feathering of lipstick and, when used all over the lips as a base, they help your lipstick to last longer. Liner can be used to alter shape if you have uneven lips.

When applying your lip liner, we would advise that you always work upwards from the corners of the mouth up to the Cupid's bow. By working upwards you will instinctively create a more rounded, natural shape.

If you don't want to create the sharp edge that a lip liner gives, then you can also purchase clear, wax-based lip liners. These will prevent your lipstick from feathering out but won't give you the liner look.

CORRECTING LIP SHAPE

By altering your lip shape you can change the whole look of your mouth. Fuller lips are not something either of us were blessed with naturally but we have both learnt how to apply liner and concealer to give us whatever shape we desire. Brands that shout about the amazing lip-plumping properties of their products generally use models with naturally fuller lips. Don't be fooled!

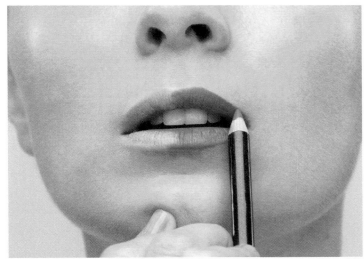

If you want to correct your lip shape then follow these steps:

1

Ensure the lips are free of dry skin and have had a balm applied to moisturise, then blot off any excess moisture.

2

Using a soft, fluffy brush, buff your regular creamy concealer over the lips and your surrounding lip area.

3

Think about colour. If you are wearing a dark lipstick you can use a matching dark lip liner but if you are wearing a nude lipstick then use a lip liner in an a stoney colour. One which has an almost grey or beige tone will work the best.

4

There is a faint white line that occurs naturally around your lips. This is the line to draw up to. Anything drawn over this line will start to look a little like a pantomime dame!

5

If you are just altering the shape and trying to make your lips symmetrical then do it in small feathery strokes, mimicking the side that you are trying to copy.

6

If you are struggling to see the ideal shape then fill in your whole lip with the liner first, which will make it easier to notice any uneven edges.

7

Ensure you use a pointed lip brush to get into all the corners of the mouth and keep to the edges of the new lip shape.

LIPSTICKS

When we worked on make-up counters, we found helping a customer to choose their desired lipstick texture and colour was a very difficult task. The colour of lipstick you choose to wear is so personal. You can apply a fabulous tomato red to a woman's lips, making her blue eyes sparkle and lifting her whole skin tone, but if she isn't used to the vibrancy then all she will see in the mirror is a huge pair of lips.

But, if you are someone who tries a lot of colours on in a store, then we would advise limiting yourself to trying three shades. Trying multiple colours will only aggravate the lips and cause them to become red, which will then affect the colour of the lipstick you are trying on.

When choosing lipstick, you also need to think about the texture. This can affect the colour intensity, how it applies and how it feels on the lip, as well as the longevity.

MOISTURISING LIPSTICKS

A sure-fire way to tell if what you're looking at is a moisturising lipstick is to look at it in the light. It will have sheen over it and also when tested on the back of your hand it will feel softer and reflect the light through its wet-look finish.

The advantages of moisturising lipsticks are that they look glossy and fresh, they feel more creamy and they won't get stuck in dry skin on the lips. The disadvantages are that they won't last very long, you'll need to touch up throughout the day, they will transfer onto your cup or whomever you are kissing, and the colour pigment in a moisturising lipstick is diluted by the various oils in the lipstick, ruining punchy, bold colours.

PH LIPSTICKS

These are lipsticks whose colour depends on your individual skin pH. They apply almost transparent, but after a few seconds the product mixes with your natural oils and acidity in the skin and changes colour, almost like a mood ring for the lips!

The colour is normally a natural wash rather than a punchy, opaque finish and they often have a moisturising, glossy texture and finish.

LIP GLOSS

Lip gloss can be worn alone or on top of lipstick. It provides a reflective shine and is easy to apply. While you may have expectations of a gloopy, sticky film, gloss is quite often smooth and balmy. All of these bounce the light off your lips and provide various finishes in the same way that lipsticks do.

There is no way of really keeping a gloss on the lips for long periods of time, as their texture is always quite wet, which means they transfer and move easily.

Lip gloss has an application wand in the lid and it can either be a brush or a doe foot-style applicator. They both do the same job really, but the doe foot drags the skin a little more.

MATTE LIPSTICKS

These have zero shine and they feel dryer on the lips. Because the colour pigment isn't diluted by any moisture, they will provide the strongest colour pay-off and we love their vibrancy. They tend to last the longest on the lips and are the best texture to choose for a long-lasting lip. Definitely the best finish if you don't have time to keep touching up.

SATIN LIPSTICKS

The satin finish in these is usually provided by a fine reflective pigment, which is infused into the colour rather than the oils and waxes, as with a moisturising lipstick. Satin lipsticks will last longer on the lip, won't transfer quite as quickly and can have a fairly intense colour.

LIP GLOSS CAN BE WORN ALONE OR ON TOP OF LIPSTICK. IT PROVIDES A REFLECTIVE SHINE AND IS EASY TO APPLY.

★★★ TIP ★★★

If you want to add colour to the lips after the gloss has worn off then put a lip-liner base on your lips first.

WHEN *CHOOSING* LIPSTICK, YOU ALSO *NEED TO THINK* ABOUT THE *TEXTURE*. THIS CAN *AFFECT* THE *COLOUR INTENSITY*, AS WELL AS *THE LONGEVITY*.

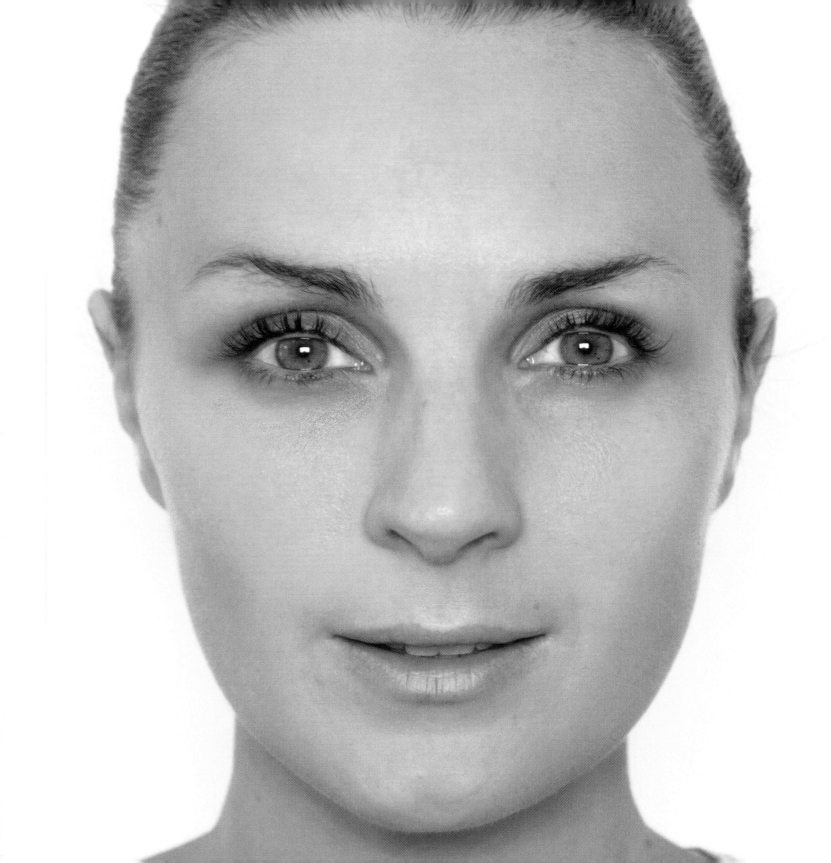

A REALLY *OLD-FASHIONED* PRODUCT. *ANYONE* WHO *GREW UP* IN THE *1980s WOULD HAVE* HAD A *LITTLE* VIAL OF *LIPSTICK-SEALING* LIQUID.

LIPSTICK SEALER

A really old-fashioned product. Anyone who grew up in the 1980s would have had a little vial of lipstick-sealing liquid. It never really worked that well and dried the lips out terribly, but since then they have improved the quality. We just prefer to layer our lip products with a liner first and then lipstick in order to achieve longevity.

LIP PLUMPERS

These apply in the same way as a gloss and can be tinted or clear. They basically work by irritating the lips. Ingredients such as pepper, caffeine or cinnamon will stimulate the blood supply to the lips and this increased circulation will cause the skin of the lips to flush and puff slightly.

They work pretty quickly, never really feel that comfortable and the effect wears off after around 15 minutes. You would need to reapply regularly to maintain the plumped effect.

We don't really like the new lip-plumping cups. The method can cause the delicate blood vessels under the skin to rupture, leaving the lips looking purple or bruised.

LIP STAINS

These are available in a few styles. Some of the slightly more old- fashioned varieties are a liquid stain in a bottle, which has a brush applicator in the lid. As the liquid dries off, it shrinks the skin underneath, giving a puckered-lip effect. They never really feel that comfortable on the lip, although the colour often lasts well.

The superior style of these are dual-ended. To use, ensure the lips are completely dry and then apply a thin layer of colour. Leave to dry and then apply the gloss coat. You will not need to touch up the staining colour but you will need to re-apply the gloss coat throughout the day.

The gloss will keep the colour moisturised and prevent cracking, though these are not the best choice of lipstick for a dry lip. The stain clings to the dryness and gives an almost bobbled finish.

LIPSTICK *COLOUR* CAN BE *VERY* PERSONAL. BUT CERTAIN *COLOURS* *WILL BENEFIT* DIFFERENT *SKIN, HAIR AND* *EYE COLOUR.*

LIPSTICK COLOUR CHOICE

Lipstick colour can be very personal, but certain colours will benefit different skin, hair and eye colour. Here are our hints and tips:

Don't be afraid to experiment with your lip colours. We quite often mix two shades together or use a contrasting lip liner colour underneath to create a unique shade. And there's no reason why you can't mix shades and textures from different brands.

However, don't share your lipsticks; they can harbour bacteria, which is easily transferred. Cold sores are the biggest concern with this and once you have one you may then always suffer from them, so be careful.

Some people say only ever make up one feature, either your eyes or your lips, but remember there are no rules in make-up. Wearing a bold look on both the eyes and lips can sometimes look overpowering but if you want to then go for it. Our everyday go-to look is natural eyes with a little of our bronzer through the socket, a black feline flick for the day and then a full-on vibrant lipstick added for the evening. It's a fail-safe day-to-night look that never dates.

NUDE LIPSTICK

Nude can be pink, brown or peach in muted, natural tones. Anyone can wear nude but the tone choice will be the difference between looking washed out or like a 1960s throwback (unless that's the look you were aiming for).

In terms of texture, a matte shade will have an opaque finish and will show up any skin texture. A moisturising or satin finish will look radiant and fresh.

If you have pale skin, choose warmer nudes rather than cool-toned ones. On a medium- to deeper-coloured skin, you can get away with most nude tones.

PINK LIPSTICK

If you are fair skinned then don't choose a pink with too much red in it; rosy-pinks or lilac- and blue-tinged pinks will suit better.

Those with olive- and medium-toned skin can pull off most shades of pink but vibrant tones will look particularly amazing. If your skin tone is deeper, then don't go too light with your pinks, as they can look a little dated if they are too pale. Candy pinks through to deep magentas look stunning.

RED LIPSTICK

Every woman needs to own a red lipstick. There is something about red that gives an air of luxury and glamour. If you fancy wearing a red but want a toned-down version then choose a moisturising red lipstick, as the moisture will dilute the colour pay-off.

Cherry reds or reds with a blue base will enhance white, which will make your teeth look Hollywood-white. Orange-reds or tomato-based reds look amazing on all skin tones, including the very fair.

BERRY/PLUM LIPSTICK

Deeper purples may not be for everyone but they look great on a darker skin tone and also make blue or green eye colour pop.

★★★ *PIXI TIPS* ★★★

[LIPS]

1 A dry toothbrush is a great tool on slightly moisturised lips for removing dry, dead skin. Using a soft bristle brush in small, circular motions will exfoliate off the dry skin.

2 Never wind your lipstick bullet up fully for application. If it's been wound up to much then it's more likely to snap or at least weaken.

3 When applying, ensure you open your mouth really wide and fill in the very corners of the lips. Often these little spaces at the edge of the lips get forgotten and will look very obvious when you're smiling or laughing.

4 If you use liner all over your lips, be sure to go for a colour similar to your lipstick. This way, when your lipstick wears off you will still have the colour from the liner showing through.

5 After applying lipstick, pop your index finger in your mouth and close your lips around the finger. When you slide your finger out you will remove any lipstick that's on the inside of the lips.

6 Dusting a loose translucent powder over your lips and then re-applying another layer of colour will help your lipstick stay in place longer. The powder will absorb any moisture on the lips which may cause the lipstick to move.

7 If you live in a hot country or are going on holiday then purchase a small lipstick case to protect your lipstick and stop it from melting or going soft in the heat.

First, we would like to say a massive thank you to all of our followers, who have supported us
on this crazy and exciting journey. Without you it wouldn't be possible. X

Thank you: Gleam Futures our fantastic management. You're the best of the best; it's rare to find managers
that really and truly has the best interests of their clients at heart. You look after us so well.
Dom, Francesca, Abigail, Viv and all the rest of the team, it's an absolute honour and pleasure to have your
help and get to work with you daily. (Also Sam apologises if anyone is ever offended by the overuse
of swearing in her emails.)

Thanks to Dundas communications: Max, Amy, Freya, Callum and Nancy for helping to steer us
in the best direction. Just like Gleam, you are a rare find.

Thanks to Blink for all your help with this book.

Thanks to our family: Mum, Ian, Steff, Danny, Brian, Lily, Ollie, Harry and Edie for supporting,
entertaining and helping us along the way. Your positive attitude when times get hard always pulls
us through and your help managing and juggling the children has been paramount to our success.

Thank you to our friends James Lincoln (for taking photographs with zero direction) ★,
Simon Songhurst ▲ and Elisabeth Hoff ♦ for all their stunning photographs without which,
this book would be rather dull to look at.

Thanks to Danny and Steve at Type & Numbers for designing this book so beautifully.

Thanks to Stacey for helping us with this book and being the best friend anyone could ask for.
May the Armchair Detectives live on forever!

Thank you to Amy for eating all the biscuits, chocolates, marshmallows, cake pops,
macaroons and sweets that come with the daily Pixiwoo post, so that we don't have to.
We'll pay for your dental bills when your teeth fall out!

Pixiwoo

After both finding careers in the make-up industry, sisters Nic and Sam joined together to create the Pixiwoo brand. Their highly successful YouTube make-up channel has over two million subscribers, each video generating hundreds of thousands of views. Sam and Nic are the faces of the famous Real Techniques brush collection, the brand has taken off in the US, the UK and around the world. Sam and Nic continue to grow as top artistic consultants, writing columns for national magazines and newspapers, appearing on major network television as beauty experts, and editing their own digital magazine. They continue to develop their Pixiwoo brand through their YouTube tutorials, as well as doing make-up courses from their studio.